MARRIED TO A NARCISSIST

Enduring the Struggle and Finding You Again

Catenya McHenry

Illustrations by Aja Marie

Narcissist- a person who is overly concerned with his or her own desires, needs, or interests.

–Merriam Webster

No part of this book may be reproduced or transmitted in any form or by any means, electronic or mechanical, including scanning, photocopying, recording, or by any information storage and retrieval system, without permission in writing from the publisher.

Copyright © 2018 by Catenya McHenry. All rights reserved.
Married to a Narcissist: *Enduring the Struggle and Finding You Again* published by **Triumph Press**
info@TriumphPress.com

Triumph Press is a resource for those who have the passion to tell their life-stories and change the world. If you have a true and inspiring story to share, visit *www.TrimphPress.com* to learn how we can help you publish and join our library of inspirational books.

ISBN-13: 978-1981641864
ISBN-10: 1981641866
10 9 8 7 6 5 4 3 2 1

To My Children:

*Emmanuel, Xavier & Alessandra
- because of you, I have no regrets*

CONTENTS

INTRODUCTION- I Can't Believe I Lived Through It 1

Part One: Journaling the Journey

MARRIAGE

    Marriage 13

    Alone 17

    All You See is You 19

    Curiosity 21

    You Have Two Cars 23

    Help Me 25

    You Don't Have to Do Anything 27

    Lost Days 29

    Ribbon in the Sky 31

    Mercedes Half Marathon 33

    The Jester 35

    Prom 37

    The Weight of a Soul 39

    I'm in Love with Someone Else 41

    Was it Just an Emotional Affair? 43

    "It's Not What You Think…" 45

    I Wish 47

    You Murdered My Soul 49

    You Took the Wrong Job 51

Pampered Chef 55
The First Time I Tried to Leave 57
Rock Bottom 59
Overcoming 61
Your Invisible Departure 65

SEPARATION
Fight or Take a Walk 71
Sometimes You're Better Off 73
Better 75
New Reality 77
Dismembered 79
My Five Years of Failure 81
The Restoration 83
What I Miss Most 85
Staying for The Children 87
To My Children 89
Stripped 91
More of Today 93
Will 95
The Smile Left My Face 97
Realization 99
Adversity 101
The Juxtaposition of Hardship + Humor 103

DIVORCE
A Whole Year 107

The Same Person 109
The Two-Year Failure 111
Tenure 113
Stubborn 115
Penmanship 117
His Last Name 119
Signing Day 123
Vortex 125
There Was a Time 129
The Ring 133
Marriage. What is it Good For? 135
The Bag Lady 137
It Still Hurts 139
I'm Not Ok 141
Letting Go 143
Don't Be Mad 147
Love's Lost 149
I Want to Hate You 151
Grieving Children 155

Part Two: Lessons Learned

The Sad Rich Girl 161
Anger 163
Bad Mom 165
Beware: They Will Unravel 167
You're A Fucking Idiot 169

Truth 171
Within Reason 173
Weak 175
Sometimes You have to Lose the Battle to Win the War 179
Stay Above the Fray 185
Zap Their Power 189
Let Them Be 193
Turtles 195
Will It Ever Stop 197
Hope and Healing 203

Resources 205
About the Author 207
Aknowledgements 209

There is no greater agony than bearing an untold story inside you.

- Maya Angelou

Introduction:
I Can't Believe I Lived Through It

The unsettling reality of being married to a narcissist is you never know what will suddenly make them snap into a cosmic realm of a false reality. Situations that seem normal and a reasonable way to handle things will be completely opposite to them. Their response to events and everyday life happenings will be so shocking, you'll be left speechless. They're sociopaths who don't think like reasonable people and they can't function unless they see themselves. If they can't see themselves or see how something will ultimately benefit them, then their behavior is spastic, wild, juvenile, and overall erratic, but they'll accuse you of being erratic. It's rather hard to explain to someone that hasn't experienced this first hand, but to someone co-existing with a narcissist, you know exactly what I'm describing.

Over time, I settled into a silent cocoon because I never knew what would upset him and make him turn on me. I stopped telling him things because I was afraid of how he would react and ultimately, I wouldn't say anything because I didn't know if I would upset him and I wasn't strong enough to not be afraid.

One of the major red flags that is incredibly memorable and poignant was raised in pre-marital counseling. I mentioned to my pastor that I was concerned that his drinking was problem and could be one in our marriage, and that I thought my fiancé was an alcoholic. My pastor brought it up during one of our sessions and boy did I get a verbal lashing afterwards in the parking lot.

As we were getting into our cars, he yelled at me with such fiery hatred, I was completely taken aback. He was jabbing his finger, telling me I had no business bringing up "his business" to my pastor. Yes, that was my first red flag, but I was so beaten down, I thought I had done something wrong and I believed him when he told me I should've kept my mouth shut and I should've never said anything.

My next devastating recollection was when I got into a car accident. Seven months pregnant with my first child, a lady sideswiped the front end of my little Miata. I was shaken and terrified for my baby. While I wasn't physically injured, I immediately called him to tell him what happened. I was not prepared for his response. I was expecting he would respond like my Dad would have if it was my Mom in a car crash. My Dad would drop everything he was doing and practically get into another accident racing to the scene. Not my ex.

He told me, "Why are you calling me? Call the police. Besides, I can't come right now, I'm in the middle of an experiment." *Wait... What??* Thinking he didn't really hear what I said, I told him again I was in an accident and I would like for him to come. After all, I was 7-months pregnant, driving a little Miata. I had to actually tell him, I'd like for him to come to the scene. WHAT??? Thankfully, my sister was with me, otherwise I would've been alone. My neighbors happened to be driving by and stopped to see if I was ok and offered to stay with me until he got there. They asked me if he was coming. I told them about my phone call and that I wasn't sure if he was coming. They were visibly in disbelief and didn't know what to say.

Nearly 30 minutes went by and still no husband. I called him again and asked him if he was coming. In a very flippant voice, he told me he couldn't stop what he was in the middle of, but he would try to come. He didn't show up until I was later loaded into the ambulance and under monitor observation for the baby's heartbeat.

After the ER technicians confirmed the baby's heartbeat, they suggested taking me to the hospital for further observation and possible tests. They told me I didn't have to ride in the ambulance, but that my husband or sister should take me. Once he realized my sister was available, he left me in her care and went back to work. *OMG!*

My sister and I were at the hospital for hours. I was admitted for half the night. Of course, I called him again to let him know I'd been admitted, but he never showed up at the hospital.

My sister took me home and there he was, lying on the couch, watching television. Never once did he call to check on me and never did he come to the hospital to see if I or the baby was ok. I was worn and went straight to bed without conversation.

This was his response to countless situations during our marriage. Nothing could prepare me for the neglect my soul, my being, my heart, and my entire existence would experience.

Over time, I learned not to tell him anything and definitely not share my feelings. Time and again, I would be met with scold, shame, and general neglect. In his world, nothing I did was right and nothing I said was right and the way I felt about something was wrong from his perspective. I was told that I needed to change and I was silly for thinking a certain thing and I was de-humanized in so many ways. I asked him to help me with the baby, just so I could take a nap or take a shower. I was shamed for even asking.

I learned to be silent and cry on the inside. My heart cried. My nerves cried. My blood cried.

This book is for those who have no one to tell. This is for those who cry inwardly. This is for those who, like me, didn't know that it was okay to leave. This is for those who believed "till death do us part" was physical death. Death do us part could also mean death of your soul. My soul was dead for years- too many that I couldn't count anymore. I was only alive because my heart told itself to beat, then beat again. That's all it did was beat, without feeling, without life, without it's organs participating.

This collection is for those who haven't found their voice, their strength, their courage and most importantly, themselves outside of their significant others. This is for those who are lost in someone else's dreams, narcissism, hopes, desires, abuse, addictions, hatred, jealously, resentment, anger, selfishness, betrayal, lies, and loveless existence. This is for those who feel like they disappear in someone else's eyes. This is for those whose children hear them cry and wonder if those are sad tears or happy ones.

My soul became mute because the narcissism was deafening. The only thing listening was my journal, as recorded in *Journaling the Journey*, Part One of this book. Writing it was not hard because it was my reality. The emotions, the pain, the sadness, it all spilled out onto the page- it's all I had and the accidental chapters kept piling up. Realizing that this was a book and not just a collection of diary entries, but what I actually lived, was the excruciating part. The emotions are raw and some are still there. The sadness is there to an extent, but the calcification of my heart, the ability to trust and the fear and desire of wanting to do this again is the collateral damage I harbor.

While finding the words and ideas for this book were not a strain, reading it, seeing the memory, and knowing I was alone through all of it is what's heartbreaking.

My cache of raw writing is what I penned because I had no one else to talk to. I had no one else to tell and at the time, I knew no one else that could relate to the horror I was enduring. I wrote because my pen and the page were my best friends and my solace. There was no peace in the pen and page because every time I gripped the two, there was more pain to pen. There are things no one knows except me and them.

I went through it all alone. No one knew what was happening. I didn't know how to talk about it. I didn't want to talk about it because I felt panicked and helpless. I didn't know how to even bring it up and if I did, how could anyone help me? I figured I would be advised to get out, but how in the world do you do that? People offer well-intentioned advice about how you should handle a situation. They have tons to say, but are they there to help you with the same fervor and energy that they gossiped about you with? No. People are dealing with their own hardships and so I tried to handle mine. Taking care of my children, work, running, and him being passed out often, were my distractions from what was happening.

I sometimes look away and stop short of reading an entire chapter in *Journaling the Journey*. It's too emotional. How could I have gone through that? How could I have lived in that; and how did I survive? It's a wonder, but I did. I also realize that some people are and have lived in worse. I'm thankful for my internal strength and the extra strength God gave me. I'm thankful for those who quietly prayed for me. I'm thankful for a system that allows you to get out of an abusive existence, but getting out doesn't mean the abuse disappears. Narcissists try hard to continue their abuse, especially if they know where you are and because of your children, they usually do know where you are.

Part Two, *Lessons Learned* further highlights the destructive evolution of the relationship and my escape from harm's way. The clarity of heart, mind, and soul taught me better ways to deal with the abuse, including how to regain my strength and find inner peace. Through my pain and sorrow, I hope it can bring comfort to you. You *will* live. You *will* survive. You *will* find you again; and you will be okay. You will be okay. This body of work is not intended to be sad. It is reality, it is raw, it is pure, it is what's true and it is life living with a narcissist. On the other side of the pain is a happier life to live, is hope to experience and real joy to share with others. It may not seem like you will survive this right now, but my story is real and I'm still here. God will give you friends who listen. The phrase you need to see on any given day could be on a post and that helps you get to the next day. It's not serendipity, it's God.

He could put you in a parking lot with your children after school one day, where you randomly meet a new friend. Your daughters could begin talking and playing and then you meet the mother of that little girl. After one minute in the conversation, you realize, you share the same experiences and were married to the same narcissistic personality. She could become one of your dear friends who helps you heal.

You could meet a new colleague on-line and realize you too have the same personal experiences, but her ex is more abusive than yours. Meeting her is not serendipity, that's God. She could become another of your dear friends who helps you heal, who encourages you and who reminds you of how strong you are and that you will get through.

He could give you a best friend who calls you every single day. If not every day, every other day. He doesn't have to say anything on the other end. What he's telling you with a phone call, and not a text, is that he cares and he loves you.

These friends, along with a host of other earthly angels that become your sisterhood network, could be poured into your life years after you sign the dotted line but, never-the-less, the healing is a continual process.

You WILL get exactly what you need and there is healing when you let go of the anger and mend the brokenness. It may take a while and that's ok. It may take years to let go, and that's ok. You can move forward when you're ready. When you find you, you can begin to make a way to find your freedom.

You'll eventually realize the amount of inner strength you have, and its power to bring you back to yourself. If you don't believe in God, you should. My belief and faith is how I can now write and share this book without drowning in the ocean of my own tears.

I hope this body of work will give you healing and hope and help you know you are not alone. This too shall pass.

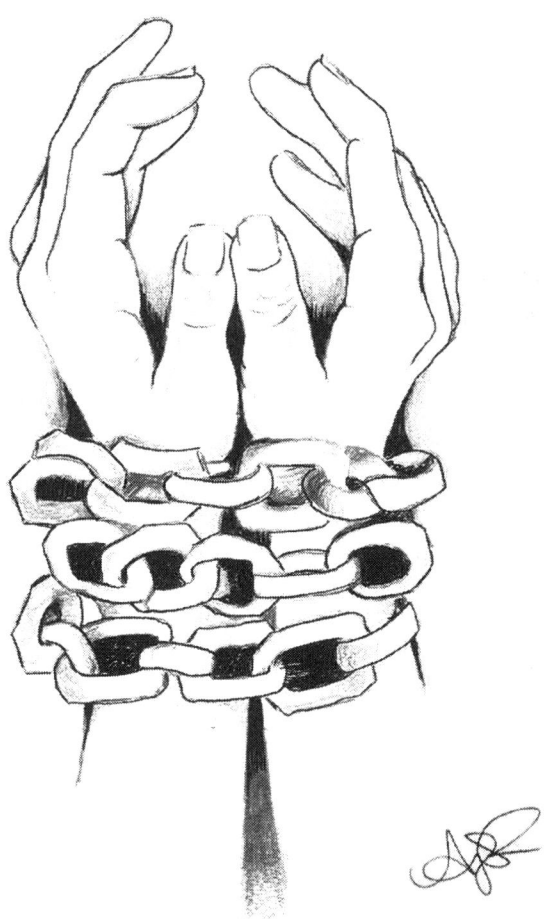

Part One
Journaling the Journey

MARRIAGE

The most stupid thing in the world is to allow yourself to be treated as NOTHING by the person you treated as your EVERYTHING.

- author unknown

Marriage

It's hard to know where to begin. Our wedding day was one of the happiest days of my life. We made so many promises to each other that at the time seemed so meaningful and effortless to keep. Now, I'm not so sure.

I just need some time away to think things through and be with God. I feel like I've drifted and need to find myself in Him again, with a renewed spirit.

I know we're both stressed and I know that we both have so many expectations of each other. Maybe it's unwise to have too many or even one expectation of your partner. I don't know. I don't know fully how to be married. I know I'm becoming less tolerant of things. I haven't learned how to talk to you, to make you listen and really understand, and "see" from my perspective how I'm really feeling. I don't know how to do that yet. Right now, telling you how I feel only makes me feel worse. It turns into being about you, how you feel, and your perspective.

I would've hand-written this to you but, well, you know, with my so-called horrible handwriting and all….

I don't feel that you're always truthful with me and I was sooo very hurt to discover what I found that I included with this letter. What am I, your wife, supposed to think or feel? What do you think goes through a partner's mind when something like this surfaces? Turn the table and think about how you'd feel if I was sending little flirty messages to someone who's claiming to be unfaithful with her husband, and here my husband is sending things like this to someone he may or may not know.

I don't know what to think about you right now. I can't trust you right now. I know that much. Suddenly, I am thrust back to what ended our relationship/friendship the first time. Am I the stupid one for marrying you? Am I? It feels really weird and uncomfortable to have you up late at late doing *whatever* while I'm asleep. It's obvious there's something going on. It's rare that we go to bed together, let alone fall asleep together. I think that's a problem. I feel like you're leading this secret life or something; call it crazy, call it intuition.

There is plenty of love here, but I can't bring a child into this environment. There's no way. On the inside, I'm not happy. On the surface, everything may look fine. But you know, what's the point? It's hard to remember a time when I've been truly, truly happy.

I can't wait around to find out what other surprises are in store for me. It doesn't take me long to catch on. I don't know how long I'll be away. Maybe I'll decide to stay away, maybe I'll come back, who knows. I just know, right now, I can't be here. I need to think about the rest of my life. If I don't, no one will.

Please understand I'm not trying to hurt you. I just need some time.

Being alone is scary, but not as scary as feeling alone in a relationship.

- Amelia Earhart

Alone

I feel more alone than I've ever felt before. It's so quiet. The children are asleep. Their father is drunk and passed out, and it's just me sitting here watching TV, trying to hold back tears. Some would say this is the perfect time to talk to God. It is.

But what do I say? I don't even know where to start. I'm completely overcome with anger, frustration, disgust, and I'm just "over" everything. I'm ready to just bust out of here.

All You See Is You

All you see is you. You live your life for you. "I" have two cars. What do you think "I" should get on "my" license plate?

It's all about you. It's all about "I." You don't live your life for them. You live it for you. You didn't even know your 3 ½-year-old doesn't like to wear shorts. Where the fuck have you been? You can't figure out why he's screaming bloody murder when you decide to pull out a pair of shorts for him to wear in the dead of winter.

He's smarter than you, you moron. He's smarter than you, and he's not even three feet tall.

Curiosity

Have some every once in a while. Wonder, for god's sake. Wonder what your children are doing when you hear the commotion. Come see for a bit and investigate.

Fucking show up for crying out loud. Engage, ask questions, wonder about other people. Be mindful. Want to know. Want to know. Figure it out. Your curiosity is in The Dead Sea along with all else that floats and lacks wonder. Selfish son of a bitch!

You Have Two Cars

While I struggle every fucking day to get the children in and out of a small car with three car seats,

    you have two cars.

While I scrape my hand and wrist buckling them each into their car seats,

    you have two cars.

As I lose skin twice a day from forcing my hand in between a tiny space, blindly navigating the seat belts into their buckles,

    you have two cars.

Hope you're happy. You have two cars, and neither of them have car seats.

Indifference and neglect often do much more damage than outright dislike.

- J.K. Rowling

Help Me

You let me do it all while you pulled up a chair or took a break on the couch, playing with your phone, while the chaos happened around you.

You are a watcher, not a doer. You sit by and watch things happen while more ambitious people around you take responsibility and do it. If it doesn't benefit you or has anything to do with you, you're the least bit interested. You fucking lazy, no good, selfish prick. God, how could your parents raise someone like you who is so wrapped up in his own ass he can't see anything but his own shit? You know it's shit, but to you, it looks and smells wonderful. There couldn't possibly be anything wrong. You don't even see it as shit. You arrogant bastard, who thinks his shit don't stink. You pompous bastard!

You Don't Have to Do Anything

All you have to think about is you. By the time you wake up, everything is done. The house is empty. Our three children, "The Trio," are taken care of, and none of your concern. They are:

    cleaned

    fed

    clothed

    teeth brushed

    hair brushed

    face washed

    Cat boo boo removed

    Homework done

    Read to

    Talked to

    Bundled up

    Snapped into the car

    Dropped at school

    Kitchen's clean

    Sheets are in the wash

    Trash is taken out

Bills are paid

Mail is picked up and sorted

All you had to think about was what "you" were going to wear today. When you do take the trash out after being asked to, you miss the truck.

So, the can sits there on the curb for two days, waiting for the next pick up day. Fucking, man-up, cause you suck.

Lost Days

4th of July. Another weekend lost to oblivion. You had no idea we were gone, even after I told you that I was taking the children to the pool. Five hours later, you didn't remember me telling you. When you finally came to you asked, "where were you guys?" You immediately fell back into unconsciousness. We went to see the fireworks. It's so sad. You were again lost, floating, gliding, shuffling.

I can't even look at you let alone talk to you or even hear your voice. Ugh!! So pathetic, so lost, such a loser. You make me so furious, so angry, so disgusted. Of course, this is not the first time. Not the first time. It's just another few days to you but actually, when you're drinking, time stops, days are nothing and hours don't exist. When will this be over? Oh my god!!!!!! I can't WAIT!!!!!!

You've missed so many moments, so many holidays, so much wasted time lost to your addiction. This is not the first time and certainly not the first days you've missed. Asshole!

Beware of the heartless who make your heart beat quickly. They're just using yours because theirs won't start.

- author unknown

Ribbon in the Sky

How is it that I just had a moment of sadness? I'm watching the Stevie Wonder special. He's singing Ribbon in the Sky. It was our first dance song at our reception. I was never more in love with him than that day and night. I remember how much my heart was not my own. It was a puddle of love. It had melted. He had it, and I don't think he knew how much of a silly puddle I was for him. It was a slow decline from that night on but those moments were incredibly surreal. My world had no sadness in it, at that moment. All I could see was peace, joy, and the purity of love.

I've never felt love like that since then. My children being born brought out a different kind of love, but deep love that comes along with giving away your entire being, heart and soul, is a different kind of love. It's unrestricted, uninterrupted, unbound by anything. It's free-flowing and knows no stubbornness. That kind of love is hard to do-over and hard to do more than once. If it's not understood, the person giving it is devastated and heart-broken. Heartbreak is an understatement. It's not understood unless the experience is shared.

Mercedes Half Marathon

You knew it was something really important to me, but that didn't matter. You started drinking and got drunk anyway. I think you did it on purpose- once again trying to keep me from accomplishment and once again was drunk the entire weekend. There was no way I was going to miss something else or cancel my plans once again because you were drinking and drunk. I couldn't do it anymore.

The race was Sunday morning. That Saturday, as you crashed into walls and fell down the stairs. I called my Dad hysterically crying that I was desperate and asked if the children could come for the weekend because, once again, their father was incapacitated. My parents talked. My Dad called me back and said they would be happy to help. I immediately packed their things and drove three hours to meet my Dad. Then I drove another three hours, all in the same day, determined I wasn't going to miss the race. I got a hotel room. Got some rest. Got up the next morning at 5:00. I couldn't sleep. I ran that race with such a heavy heart… immersed in heartache and emotion.

I finished. I finished. I have a medal to prove it. The deeper meaning of finishing is still being realized.

The Jester

I remember the day when I realized that you couldn't make me happy. I don't remember the exact day, but I guess I remember the realization. The realization was cosmic. Maybe I always knew it, but again, it was my hope and my positivity about everything that conveyer belted me forward. I knew it because you didn't make me happy.

The flowers and good-will made you happy because you thought your fake was blanketed. You thought Blue Mountain cards covered up your core. You thought your *other* person was being noticed. You know, the one you created just for this relationship. He really wanted to exist, and he did, but he couldn't make the facade last long enough because he wasn't that smart. He wasn't that intelligent. He couldn't figure out two moves ahead and stay there.

He was not the fool. You are. You were. You are. You will be. You always are. Fools dance in the courtyard. Fools are seen by all. Fools play games, and when the show is over, fools go back to who they are, fools without the costume or makeup.

Prom

Drunk again. I went as a chaperone to my school's prom, but I didn't stay more than an hour. I had a weird feeling I should hurry home. Good thing I did. The house was wide open with all the lights on. It was nearly midnight, and the garage was still open. The door was unlocked, and the back door was wide open, along with the screen door. You, of course, were passed out on the couch. The children were asleep. I was so freaked out.

I thought someone had broken in. You are a danger and a harm to everyone. That was so unsafe. If someone wanted to harm the children, they didn't have to try very hard. There was an open invitation to just walk right in.

The Weight of a Soul

You are such a heavy soul and spirit. Some people can enter a room, and exuberant energy of their spirit is immediately absorbed. The room gets brighter, and the people in it are happier- filled with a burst of life.

Others, like you, can enter a room and immediately there's angst, tension, and the people in it start to squirm, fidget, get cranky, fussy, and just lose all sense of joy.

It's really astonishing that just one person can so negatively anchor and drag the spirit of a space. I hate being around that. That's what you are. Really. You see it in cartoons and everyone laughs, but you are that dark cloud- the one that changes everything to drab gray; such a blah color. It's lifeless; it's hopeless; it's just there. Its presence says everything without uttering a sound.

...above all else, guard your heart. For everything you do flows from it.

- Proverbs 4:23

I'm in Love with Someone Else

I'm in love with someone else.

You don't recover from those words.

Your soul never expected the sonic boom, so it doesn't know how to get over it. It can't.

That's not what those words do. They don't recover; they explode and obliterate.

They propel your realm into another existence that you can never get gravity from.

In that floating, they tell you, you should've known it could happen.

They lie to you, and they tell you, you're ok.

They tell you that's what love does. It doesn't prepare you for the blow because it only knew bliss and it was the bliss that blinded the potential blow, and it was the bliss that warped the truth. You saw it. You saw it when you said "I do," but you believed the lies because you were too scared to be your own savior.

Was it Just an Emotional Affair?

One of the facts that surfaced while we were dating was that he cheated on every girlfriend he ever had. Not only did he disrespect women, but he either got bored quickly or wasn't man enough to not yield to the temptation, and he had lots of self-inflicted temptations- even during the marriage.

Yes, there were red flags, but their narcissistic charm convinces you that all the unfaithfulness stops with you, and it definitely stops when you're engaged and married.

One of his ex-girlfriends, a Hurricane Katrina victim whom I felt so sorry for, came to visit on her way to a better place. I wanted to help her in any way I could. That's what we should do, right? If you have a heart, you should help another human being in any way you can, especially someone who's lost everything meaningful to them. I had no idea they apparently still had feelings for each other, or perhaps it was just him being who he is.

The reunion sparked something that eventually turned into much more than just seeing an old flame. It became months of heartbreaking discovery- finding love professing emails between the two of them, text messages, repeated phone calls to his cell and his office, and even our home. It went on for months. Eventually, he told me at lunch one day that he wanted to separate. It didn't bother him that I was three months pregnant with my third child. Rather than care about his decision and how it affected the children and me, he was so cavalier, so careless, and could crush my soul, walk away, and not look back. He even later accused me of deliberately getting pregnant.

My daughter was nearly a year old when I snapped. I decided there's was no reason to continue staying for the sake of the children. It was her being a girl that made me realize I would kill the person that dared to treat her the way he was treating me and I told him that. He left the room in silence. That gesture told me everything else I needed to see.

By this point, there was nothing to save, there was nothing to fight for, and there was nothing a counselor could mend. He told his affair, in an email, that if he and I didn't make it, he would need her and he would want her. She reciprocated. He had already moved to the next.

I'm a fighter. It's probably what fueled my strength and desire to call her. I didn't know what I was going to say, but marriage and love were so sacred to me, I had to say something. Mine had lost hope, but I still had to ask her if she really knew what she was doing. She said she was sure about how she felt, but she second-guessed her heart when I reminded her that what she was helping him do to me, is what he had done to her while they dated in college years before.

His emotional love affair had a metaphorical heart attack that day, and he was on to the next.

"It's Not What You Think..."

Mindy

Veronica

Jennifer

Danielle

Susan

Amber (college student)

Nancy

"Next..."

*The names have been changed to protect other's identities.

Evolving involves eliminating.
- Erykah Badu

I Wish

I wish you loved me more.

I wish you adored me more.

I wish you touched me more.

I wish you looked at me more.

I wish you didn't give up so easily.

I wish you would've done what you promised me you would.

I wish you had given me everything. I did that for you.

I wish you had the guts to be honest with me.

I wish you had the guts to be honest with yourself.

I wish you hadn't let me down.

I wish you could see me.

I wish you weren't blinded by you.

I wish you believed in me.

I wish you valued me.

I wish you valued my character.

I wish you exalted me.

I wish you acknowledged my character.

I wish you understood my heart.

I wish you could see my dreams and not see just you in them.

I wish for so much more from you.

I now wish for someone that will.

You Murdered My Soul

It would've been better if it were premeditated, that would at least give some insight, but it wasn't. I bled out slowly. Every hurt was a piercing stab. A few were critical life-ending stabs. Stabs to organs- they don't recover. They can be replaced, but finding new ones is a painstaking process. How ironic. You could be on the list for years before you're back. In the meantime, your soul is now a spirit floating above you, waiting to re-enter its person.

You Took the Wrong Job

❝You took the wrong job." I believed those words until a dear friend opened my eyes. "How can someone tell you that, when you're doing what you love and are passionate about?" she questioned. "That's wrong. No one can tell you that."

What she said sunk into my soul and it was the first time I actually thought about how terrible that statement was.

It took me almost a year to find a job after my second son was born, and then suddenly I had two offers to ponder, one in PR and the other in television. The public relations position paid more, but the television job is what set me alive, fueled my fibers, and gave me the strongest sense of purpose. I LOVE television. I LOVE the challenge of live TV and most of all, I love storytelling. The TV job was the natural choice, but it really wasn't a choice for me. I knew exactly what I wanted to do, but I also wanted to make sure it was right for my family.

Since I was married and he was working, I didn't think I might not be supported. After all, we uprooted our lives and moved to place I was apprehensive about so that he could pursue his dream. I never imagined I wouldn't get the same support; this was my dream-job too. I had always wanted to land a main-anchor position, and this was exactly that.

We discussed what it would mean from a scheduling stand point, since it was night hours. He'd have to do daycare pick up, dinner, bath, bedtime, and all the parenting responsibilities I was managing.

I eventually chose the television job. "That's going to change my life, and I won't be able to work late anymore," he told me. "That wasn't smart.

Everyone knows you always take the one that pays more." Those words, like so many others, are still tattooed in my brain.

My first night on the job was excruciating. I was away from my children, not able to do dinner, story time, and bath time. It was a tough adjustment. The first week ended with me in the bathroom in tears. He made it worse by asking me what was wrong and then walking out of the bathroom in silence and closing the door after I poured out my heart. His cold shoulder left me sobbing on the icy bathroom floor.

The next few weeks and months, we grew further apart as he stopped talking to me after I'd get home. He was so angry about my taking the TV job that he literally stopped speaking to me. He wouldn't even watch the newscast. I would come home, have a bowl of cereal, shower, and go to bed. The next morning, I'd get up by myself. He slept while I got the children ready and took them to daycare. He would be gone by the time I'd come back home to get ready for work.

The silent treatment was devastating. The silent treatment is devastating for most anyone, especially communicative people who like to talk through problems. He knew how to hurt me.

He also hated I was getting more attention than him. When viewers began recognizing me in public and would reach out and speak, he would act really funny- almost jealous.

The psychological stress was too much. Not only was he not speaking to me and creating distance, but he was also grooming his affair. I felt like I was the one that had to do something to fix the situation and fix my marriage. He made me feel like I had upset the entire balance in the home. Yes, I believed him. His narcissist abuse told me I caused the problem. Wanting to bring happiness back, I began looking for a PR job. I didn't last a year at the TV station, and it crushed my being to leave, but I was more obsessed with what I thought was fixing my family. I left the station and began one of the worst jobs of my entire professional career, but he was a least speaking to me again.

That job didn't last, and I was right back where I started. Someone got what they wanted, but that someone wasn't me.

Pampered Chef

I couldn't go to a team meeting tonight because once again you are drunk and I dare not leave the children in your care. You can't even take care of yourself. This is the third day you've walked around like a zombie.

I'm trying to make a living since leaving my job. I planned to sell PC. I have in the past. You've not only taken away everything, but now you're trying to take away my future, my hope, my chance to rise above. You are a parasite.

The First Time I Tried to Leave

I knew it was time to leave. I decided that was the only way to live. I told my son's pre-school teacher, at morning drop-off, that I was taking the day to apartment hunt. She cheered me on because she knew what was happening on the inside.

Searching all day, I found a fantastic space I was happy with and had enough room for the four of us and wasn't far from our house so the children could stay in the same schools.

I felt partially liberated to write the deposit check and set a move in date. My plan was to do it while he was at work, that way he couldn't railroad me and make things more difficult.

A few days later, he found the carbon copy of the deposit check. The same day he drained every penny from our bank account, which included my paycheck. He put the money somewhere secret.

Deeply ashamed and sheepishly embarrassed, I called the apartment complex to ask for my $500 deposit back. After reluctantly explaining what happened and that I was trying to leave my husband, they kindly obliged and wished me well. It was all the money I had.

He didn't want me anymore, but he also didn't want me to do better.

He sliced me at the knees.

I dragged my body, army crawling on my elbows, back to square one.

Rock Bottom

I think I've finally hit rock bottom. I have no more hope. I have no more excited anticipation for the future. My reality is the same every day; clean up, apply for jobs, try to make things happen, and at the end of the day, sadness still reigns, loneliness is blanketing my heart, and I'm left with nothing.

Why can't I just go and be free, why am I still here? He doesn't love me nor does he care, so why am I here to hear criticism about what I've done, or what I didn't do. Nothing I do is right, and what I think is good or right, he doesn't even notice. They say God sees. Why even believe that God cares. I can't seem to rise above the pain and hurt and disappointment in everything. This relationship is sad and lonely. He doesn't even tell me he loves me anymore. He doesn't even wear his wedding ring. I've given everything, all of me like I promised at the altar. I gave up my life's dream because he wasn't happy. Now, look at me! Now, look at me!

Overcoming

What hurts the most is you just don't know. You don't know what I'm going through. You don't know the pain, hurt, and sadness you've caused and continue to cause. I really feel like you don't even care. I feel like your greatest wish at the moment is to just, "be by yourself" as you've said; which is the saddest thing I've ever heard from someone who has a beautiful family like you do.

Well, you may just get your wish. All I know is just to give you what you want and move on from there.

I want to be so angry with you for causing this life-change for all of us, but being angry with you only makes me the same as you, and I refuse to make that my reality. I am learning how to make our new reality work and make sure that the children are continuously happy, and don't miss a beat. I am learning to lean on my strength and lean on God for the rest of it. It's so incredibly hard and hurtful.

I wish you could realize how astoundingly selfish you are, to only want to be by yourself. God has given you such incredible gifts, but you see them as burdens. It's too bad you are too weak to handle all that God has given you. If you had a relationship with God, you would turn to Him for what's missing in your life. Instead, you look to eliminate what's best for you. You choose to run away and ignore and turn your back on your family. It takes a strong person to face up to difficulty, and the weak run the other direction. I have felt like the last two years; I've been working so hard to make this work. I see myself chasing you as you run away, and I never catch up to you. You won't let me. You won't let me in. You won't let me around; you just won't let me be who I need to be. I know I've made so many mistakes. God has shown me, and I am in the process of recognizing that and making them right. I am human full of flaws and imperfections; I know that. You won't ever let me be imperfect. You won't ever let it be a mistake and let it go. You want to be angry and, therefore, I have become the enemy. Those on the outside looking in take sides, they don't know. They see you as the victim and it's not fair. I know who I am and I know I have a good heart and always want to make people happy. Some just don't want that though.

It's sad; you are so weak that you let people put things in your head. I wish you really took the time to think back and remember the good more than the bad, but therein lies the other problem. What "you" remember, whether or not it's reality or what really happened, is the way you remember it and again, you are the victim.

You have ignored and neglected me nearly our entire marriage. School has come first, even though you said you would "always be available for conversation even when the school work got to be too much." That was a promise you couldn't keep, and it hurts more than you'll ever know. You break my heart; you broke my heart.

I've wanted to just talk to you, just talk and let my heart speak. I've wanted just to pour out, but you stopped me all the time and made me save it till the weekend. Weekends come, weekends go, and each one you're drunk. Why talk to you then?

Years come and go, seven of them, and I still haven't talked to you. You haven't talked to me. When it has to do with school, and only then, you talk to me. But wait, you did talk to me when you told me you wanted out. You never tried. It was just easier for you to walk away.

You went to jail; I was there. The day your 18-month probation ended, you spent all day at the bar, somehow drove home, threw up in your car and then urinated in the front yard. I was there. You were in school; I was there. You started a new job; I was there. Your drinking drove me away, but I came back. You tore muscles in your knee; I was there.

You carried on with other women; I was there. You have an emotional (maybe more) affair; I was there. You all but have sex with her, or maybe you did. You turn your back on me time and time again. I was there. You walk out on me and our children; I'm still here. You drink and drink; and I was there. You have ruined my happiness and taken so much life from me because of your selfishness and drinking; I was there. You go out and drink with students; I was there, taking care of the children. You do whatever the hell you want to; I am there. You have the right and audacity to be angry with me; I am there. I've taken incredible care of you and our children, and you have the right to be angry with me, and shout and scream at me, talk down to me, belittle me, curse at me, have a bad attitude when I asked for help… and I am still there.

WHY???

Because I loved you and I said I would, because I trusted you with my heart and my soul, because I believed you and believed in you, because I believed we would work it out no matter what because we said we would. I promised you that I would.

But you have the right to betray me, lie, steal, hate, not forgive. Why does God reward the evil-doer? Why does God allow you to turn your back on your family and go on like it's just another thing, and you are walking away? Why?

Through it all, I know God will give me and the children exactly what we need to get through this incredibly difficult time. I know He will make me strong enough to raise beautiful, good people.

Your Invisible Departure

You left me first. I think it may have been more shocking and sudden if you left in-person. But your leaving was an invisible departure.

You left my soul.

You left my spirit.

You abandoned your promises.

You rolled your eyes at my tears.

You turned your back on my sorrow which drove the spear deeper and out the other side.

You silenced my voice. You stabbed me in the throat. The pain was too much to speak about. It was too much to voice. I choked on my own blood. I was choking on my own sorrow. All the while you went on.

Your departure was slow. It happened over days. It happened over hours. It happened over dinner. It happened as you lie disgusted next to me. So disgusted that if my foot crossed the invisible line in bed and touched yours, you snatched it back, kinda like what you did with your vows.

My emotions were so out of control and misplaced, they just found a new place and left me alone, leaving me numb, wilted, and unable to understand why you bricked me out.

I fought with every organ. I fought with every electrode. I fought with every cell. I fought with even the sick ones. They couldn't help me anymore. They died trying, but at least they participated; more than I can say for you.

My strength gave me life then. My strength gave me the two feet to plant. I was standing only because my legs were determined to see me through. They knew I was brittle, but that's when they showed me their power and they weren't going to let the pillars show any signs of weakness or cracks. My core is incredible. My core fought back, and my core won. Your invisible departure took its finale, but now you're back with another round of something- the revelation of your weakness.

You let us go. You let me go. You opened your hand and you didn't hold on. You opened your hand, as I dangled from the top of the Dubai tower. The look in your eye was of relief as you let go of your grip and took your invisible departure.

Married To A Narcissist

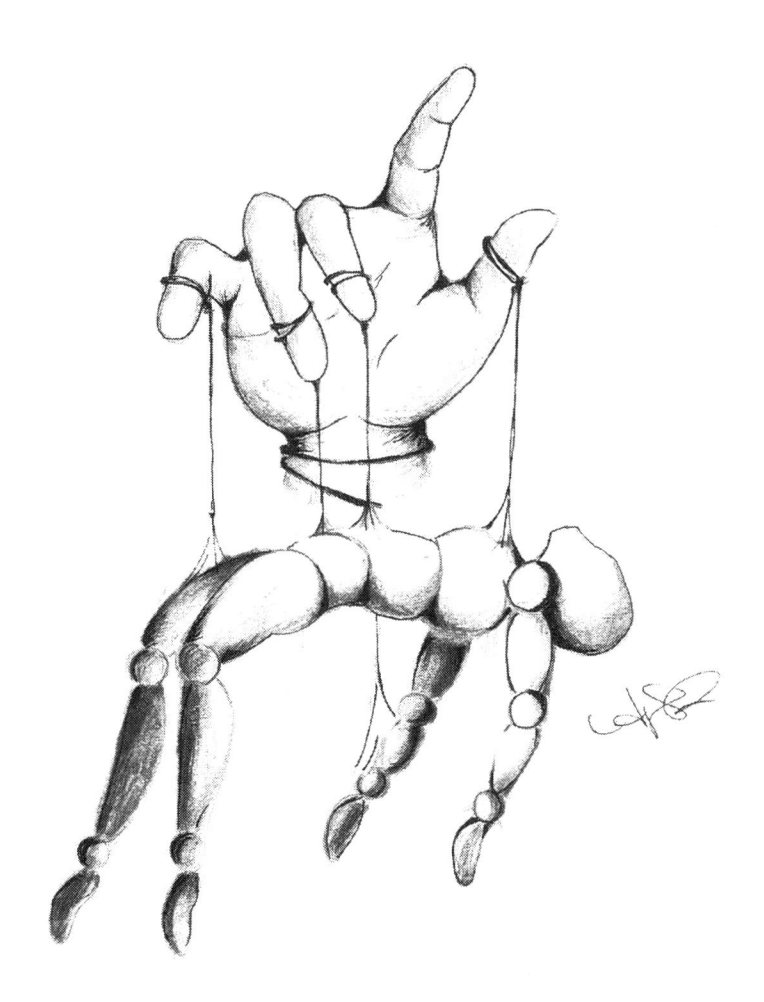

SEPARATION

There's a difference between giving up and knowing when you've had enough.

- author unknown

Fight or Take a Walk

What I know for sure today is, you have to know when it's better to fight or just walk away. For fighters, walking away is the hardest part because you feel like you failed a little. Fighters stay in till the death. Sometimes it's their own death that ends the assault.

If you truly believe the fight is worth it, and if the cause is worthy, then you stay in, and you fight to the death. But if you thought it through, and your conclusion was that nothing will change, no matter how hard you fight, then it could be better to let go, leave it, walk away and never turn back around.

Walking away will be frustrating and angering but when time takes its walk, many times it takes the stress with it and the energy spent will be but a zephyr.

Sometimes You're Better Off

Sometimes you're just better off without that thing you think you need. Sometimes, it's easier to just do and go forward on your own, instead of waiting around for the ghost to pretend he's going to show any signs of life.

Better

Happiness is so close; I can actually taste it now. I never thought I could live those words Natasha Bedingfield sings about in *Unwritten*. I'm learning to not let the anger define me and the decisions I make. I use to go to bed angry every night, and then wake up the same way. It's still there, but not every day. I'm the only one angry. I'm the only one affected by it; I finally realized that. I'm giving myself a heart attack- not anyone else… I am. So, while I looked at the pile of all your shit on the floor and I expected you would help and pitch in, while I think about all the hurt and neglect you've given, I try not to let what I see anger me. I've realized you will not change. You are always the same.

I know exactly what you're going to do, and I know exactly what you won't do. So why am I upset? Why am I angry with you? There are no surprises. None! I have to make changes to secure my own happiness and the same for *The Trio*. I am in charge of me, my destiny, my thoughts, my decisions, my dreams, my life.

I am moving on physically, emotionally, and mentally. I have already begun the process. I can do this. I am strong and thick-skinned. You are not in charge anymore. It's not about you anymore! I am internally smiling and finally getting my joy back.

New Reality

The hardest part about today is getting used to my new reality and getting used to the fact that we are a family of four and not five. I always thought I would have the same strong family bond I grew up in. I wanted and thought it would continue after I said, "I do." It didn't, and it's such a sad reality that I am the "everything" for my children. I am their caretaker. I am their strength. I am the one they depend on for everything. The beginning of the new year wasn't exciting, but rather lonely and sad. So many bad memories of 2009 are still ripe, like a newly peeled banana. I sat on the couch and by 11:45 pm, I shut everything down. But what was still on, is my new life. My new life with just me and the children. Our new family, without a father. He doesn't even know what to be or how to be a family. I'm sad that's who I said "yes" to, and even more sad that my children are growing up without him.

That's the saddest part for me is having to explain to them why their Daddy is not here when everyone else's is. Why their uncles are around, but their Dad is not. It breaks my heart every time I see the wonder in their eyes about their Dad's lack of involvement. I sometimes feel so responsible, but then I recall all the shit and remember my job to raise respectable men, even if their father is a first-rate asshole who doesn't know how to treat a lady; and who is even worse at being a husband and father. It's a hard road to walk down over cobblestones, rocks, sand, gravel, and broken glass. You almost can't avoid getting nicked, because with every step you have to look down and focus so intently that you miss what's ahead, because you can't look up. I can't look up. I can't see what's ahead. I'm more concerned now about taking each step and not losing skin.

Dismembered

The very core of you and who you are is gone. Your soul, spirit, mentality, and self-awareness are all in a different place. You recognize it's gone. All you have left is your head, your eyes with which you see the world, and all of your body parts, and that's all. You see all of your body parts scattered about and all you want to do is get them and put yourself back together again. It's not as simple as Humpty Dumpty, but is the same idea, with more complexity.

My Five Years of Failure

Nothing I did in the last five years ever caught on or gained momentum and traction. The last five years was an archive of failed attempts. They would start off great, with seemingly tip-top potential and lather, like an inviting, warm bubble bath. You watch as the tub fills, the bubbles rise, and your excitement grows with it. But, like every good bubble bath, the bubbles eventually pop, and the lather disappears, and all you're left with is dirty water- that's what life, the last five years, has been like.

First, it was my two-year project, my television show, "Nothing to Wear." Then it was my overall career and lastly my marriage. Each slowly faded.

Thinking back, they all were on the same course of demise. I just didn't know it, and I was too much of an optimist to imagine that it could ever happen to me. Maybe I should've had an emergency plan, a back-up plan, a fail-safe, a plan B, like my engineer husband. It's what engineers do, plan for the worst and "hope" for the best. But I just don't have it in me to live that way. I always have hope for the best first and tend not to plan for the worst. I always have faith that things will work out. Maybe that's why I handle disappointment so poorly, as my Mom once told me.

I'm better at handling disappointment now. I had to figure out how to find my way out of the darkness and disappointment, and let God put it all back together. I'm still not fully restored as I sit on a plane headed to LA to find myself, my joy, my purpose, my passion, my being, and most of all, my soul. I know that's where it all is.

The Restoration

The restoration began with the lack of patience and intolerance of my current situation. A spouse whose behavior and personality I tolerated because of my patience and the false idea of "for better or worse." It's really a lie. I let myself believe that to the point of losing myself. How can that be right? How can that be happiness? It's not; at least for me. I finally realized I needed and wanted better and it was okay to feel that. That feeling took a long time for me to accept… five years in fact. I guess in a sense; the last five years have been my metamorphosis. The frustration has forced me into it. The disgust has forced me into it, and my sheer will and determination and realization of my own personal power for change that has forced me into it.

Marriage tends to force couples into this alternate reality that you must do what the other wants and continually sacrifice your own needs in order to achieve and maintain harmony. Unless you write your own vows, like we did, you are coerced or forced, however you tend to see it, into saying or believing as a woman you are to submit yourself to your husband and do everything in your power to please him and he in turn provides you with all your material wants and needs and occasional emotional, sexual and mental satisfaction. Bullshit!

At this juncture, I do not believe in marriage. I believe you can have all those things you want without a spouse. I do believe in companionship and healthy close relationships with other people; I think as humans that is essential. I just don't believe that you need marriage to achieve ultimate personal bliss. My marriage, like many others, has brought about sadness, disappointment, anger, hatred, cynicism, feeling burdened, frustration, and ultimately, a strong desire for change.

It always starts off great and exciting and intriguing and then they finally let you see who they really are. Many times, that doesn't happen until after the "I do's."

What I Miss Most

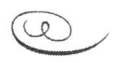

What I miss most is being in love. Truly in love. I miss looking at the other person and seeing deep love in his eyes. I miss my cheek next to his and the feeling of being in love. I miss being held. I miss being kissed softly. I miss sharing, and I miss loving the other person. There were moments of love, but not enough to sustain a lifetime relationship.

Staying for the Children

I stayed five years too long, thinking I would be the one responsible for dismantling the family unit; and I was afraid that would be too much guilt to live with. If you think you're staying for the sake of children, you're not. You're likely staying because, like me, you're too scared- scared of a myriad of things: what you'll do on your own, how will you make it on your own, how angry will your significant other be with your leaving, will the children be sad and depressed, how will you handle visitation and the drop-offs and the list of "talking yourself out of leaving" reasons.

The truth is, you're not staying for the children's sake. Thinking you don't want to break up the family or the household is a lie. It's false. The home is already broken. Love and stability are compromised.

Children know you're being abused. The abuse has not only affected you, but it's affecting your children in tangible and intangible ways. Although they may not recognize it in physical form, they see it and they feel it. They feel it when the narcissist needs to have the last word. They feel it when scenarios always come back to the narcissist. They feel it when their abused parent's face changes. They feel it when you're hiding, and hiding something.

They feel it in gestures. They feel it when the abuser lashes out. They feel it when the abuser can't hold it in anymore.

The thing about children is that they are insightful, intuitive, perceptive creatures, and they always know. You're not protecting them from anything, you're only keeping the truth from them, and that's all they want. They just want the truth and love.

They feel it when they go to school, and they can't focus. They feel it when they get in the car after school and notice your face is wrinkled from worry and fear.

Fear is that monster that sits on the edge of your shoulder whispering hateful lies; it laughs every time you flinch. It laughs every time you sigh at the end of the work day. It laughs when you stay past quitting time. It laughs every time you take the long way home… prolonging the inevitable. It laughs when it sees you believing what its said to you.

Fear is crippling, and fear is happy when you're complacent. Complacency may seem like a better state of life, but there is no change in complacency. Everything stays the same. There's only fear to keep you from a happier life. Fear is only alive when you give it life.

To My Children

I finally know what to say to you guys. I haven't known what to say about why I had to leave, and why we had to leave Daddy. I finally couldn't take the hurt and pain of loneliness. Daddy was not a good husband to me and a good father to you. He forgot about us and forgot how to make us happy.

He would tell other women things that he should've told me. We grew apart. We weren't friends anymore, and he stopped telling me he loved me. He was not a good helper. He left everything up to me, and never knew how or wanted to pitch in.

I had to live; I had to leave. I had to live; I had to leave. I had to save my own life. I had to let you guys see me be happy. I wasn't happy, and I hated who I had become. I was mean and frustrated and hateful and angry all the time. I woke and went to bed that way. I couldn't take it anymore.

We had to leave.

It was one of the hardest things that I've ever done, especially with an uncertain future. But I knew I couldn't stay. I knew we couldn't stay. I have always wanted to give you more happiness than sadness. I couldn't do it with Daddy around. He took all the happiness away. Now it's time to get it all back. I love you each so, so, so much!

Stripped

He stripped me of everything: hope, myself, my soul, my purpose, everything that I knew anything about my sanity, my joy, real love, real life, and now I just float. Now I wear a smile like lipstick or fake eyelashes. Faking Happy.

More of Today

And more of today finished dropping me to the ground level. Rejection emails from job applications every now and again are not back-breaking, but rejection daily will cripple you. How do you move, how do you breathe, how do you make a change? How do you even know what to change? How do you know what's wrong? Yes, you turn to God, but today; today, the world took a seat on my back, and today the world got tired on my knees, and today the world had nothing better to do than to take the day off, stay home in pajamas, and slouch on my soul.

Today, I couldn't come up for air. Today, insanity joined me for a cup of coffee. Today, my little girl wiped my tears. Today, my little girl told me, "It's gonna be okay." Today, my two- year old little girl brought me a Kleenex, and today my soul and spirit dissolved to liquid on the floor.

Today, I got stuck, and today everything was too loud, and today I couldn't hear my thoughts. Today my reason and capabilities took a holiday and left me with lowliness.

Today, I couldn't take anymore, and today, a simple matter was overwhelming and overloaded my systems. Today, I wanted to stop fighting and wave my homemade flag.

Today, I took it out of my bag and had it ready as my anxiety was accused of shaken baby syndrome. I couldn't see. I couldn't stop shaking.

Today... I just couldn't.

Will

Today is the first day I ever thought seriously about a will. Who would care for my children if something happened to me? I didn't even think twice or second guess my Dad. With stiff instructions though, to raise them Catholic and send them to a Catholic school and church, preferably a Cathedral. Everything and anything else needs no instruction. I know he would love them, take care of them, listen to them, play with them, give them the attention they so deserve and need.

He is the perfect role model. He is "the guy," the positive, kind man with such a beautiful spirit and a joyous heart, always a positive word. He is the one you turn to when no one else will listen. He will tell what you need to hear and what you don't want to hear and of course, what you already know. He's your audible conscience. He's in your ear with his chin on your shoulder, so gentle, so loving that you sometimes have a love and hate for him in the same moment. But he is understood, and you understand him. He loves his children more than dearly and genuinely and can't function when they hurt. That's the kind of Dad everyone needs and certainly the one my children need. He actually feels sorry for and prays for their sperm donor. How can that be? How can my Dad pray for a man that neglected his family, treated them like shit, and watched them drive away without even so much as a sweat bead of fight. My Dad has the sympathy of a strong Octavious.

Healing doesn't mean the damage never existed. It means the damage no longer controls our lives.

- Carolyn Harrington, The Art of Healing

The Smile Left My Face

I smiled only because that's what my face memorized how to do, not because there was something inside that motivated it to show itself. My face was grey then. I look back at pictures and see a much better-looking person. I was prettier, but there was a time when it just wasn't there.

My face wasn't there. The joy behind the face and eyes decomposed, as dead bodies do after a while. The decomposition was gradual. Every hurt crinkled another organ, and every discovery flattened another part until the life was fading. I was breathing only because God is not ready for me. That's all I was doing. I wasn't really forcing myself to breathe. It was automatic because, like my face, that's what it knew how to do.

I wasn't a being. I wasn't vivacious. I wasn't passionate. I couldn't even feel anything. I told my children I loved them because I did and I do, but I didn't feel it. It's what my brain was programmed to say. My heart only ticked, it didn't beat. It didn't feel. It didn't exude itself. It got really sad and recluse. It broke- at first just in half, then again in fourths, and again, again; and pretty soon it scattered into so many pieces that I got too tired to count. It gathered itself up and just sat quietly in a corner, holding onto and guarding every piece, but not knowing what to do with the pile of rubble. As time went on, the pieces began to find their places again. Like a broken bone in the toe, there's not much intervention you can do. The bone has to heal itself, it knows how.

The heart heals, and as it does, the ticks return to beats and each beat pumps new blood and new cells back to life. I look at myself now, and the smile brews from my gut before it splashes my face. I can feel it. I have a life to smile about. Every beat puts the color back, and every color is creating another painting we call life.

Realization

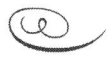

It's amazing the number of realizations that show up when you're either in the shower or just about to jump into REM sleep. In both these cases, you can't write them down right away. You can only hope your memory is nice long enough for you to find a pen or get into your iPhone.

Tonight, I realized I found my outlet, or maybe it found me. This is my outlet… writing. For so long, I've wanted a way to express myself, as a dancer does in a move or a song-writer does in music, or a painter does on a canvas. This is mine. It really happened by accident, or maybe it was nothing of the sort. I turned to the blank page because no one else would listen, really listen. When I needed to regurgitate or be sick from holding it in; I turned to the page. It was the only place to put the hurt and shame and disappointment, and frustration and the anger and the anxiety and the feeling of being lonely and, of course, the sadness. It was the only place all the misery could go. It was the only place they could all rest easy. It's the only place the cancer could remiss.

Adversity

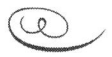

Adversity is not reserved for those that are already struggling or sad or down to their last $1. Adversity seems to tackle anyone and everyone. We often think that adversity is allergic to rich people or those who seem to have it all together. The truth is, everyone is going through something.

My Mom always told me that it was important to be kind to people and to not take things too personally, especially if someone was rude or could've treated you better. "You never know what they're going through and you never know what could've happened before you ran into them." That thought is always with me, but that doesn't mean I don't get offended by certain things or react to what may have just transpired.

Getting older and living life makes you wiser and less tolerant. So, while you're experiencing something unpleasant, your wisdom may give you better ways to handle it.

I existed in a nearly 10-year narcissistic marriage that I knew in the first year was going to be over, but I stayed, thinking that I was committed to not leaving.

Not all of it was a nightmare though. There was good and bad. The good was when I was doing exactly what the narcissist wanted. The minute my stubborn personality oozed out; there was backlash, verbal beatings, and mental massacre. I was so twisted; I lost my soul, but no one knew just how bad it was.

Through the horror, I still got dressed every day and tried to put on a good face, even though adversity was slowly feeding on my organs… no one knew. I hid it well because I believed living was what I was supposed to keep doing. I kept living, smiling, laughing, pretending that I was ok, but I wasn't ok.

The Juxtaposition of Hardship + Humor

I want to just stop. I want to just give up. I want to have a meltdown. If I did, the pressure would be relieved. The stress would be less, and I could just breathe.

Today, I received two rejection emails. It doesn't seem like much, but I get a handful each week. I apply for at least three jobs every day. One day I hit a record, ten… pretty efficient, some would say. I say pretty desperate; pretty damn desperate. What am I even good at?

What am I doing wrong? Things that match my skill-set perfectly, I'm being turned down for. How do I even do this and how do I even get past the application? What do they want? Who do they want? How do I transform into who and what they want? How much can my soul take? I want to let it loose and just cry. I want to just let the river of life slowly flow out of me. But as I sit on the couch listening to the children whispering to one another as they should be falling asleep, I'm watching television with jealousy, but am inspired at the same time. I'm jealous to see other people doing all the things I want to do. Inspired by all the things other people are doing. How do I reach that and grab that without hurting my hand on the glass? How do I achieve that? How do I do that?

How can I make it happen? I don't freaking know! Nothing I'm doing is working, but I keep the pursuit. I am tired, but energized by my children and the funny things they say, the things they see as funny. In the midst of hardship, it's the funny little things that can shimmer a glimmer of hope.

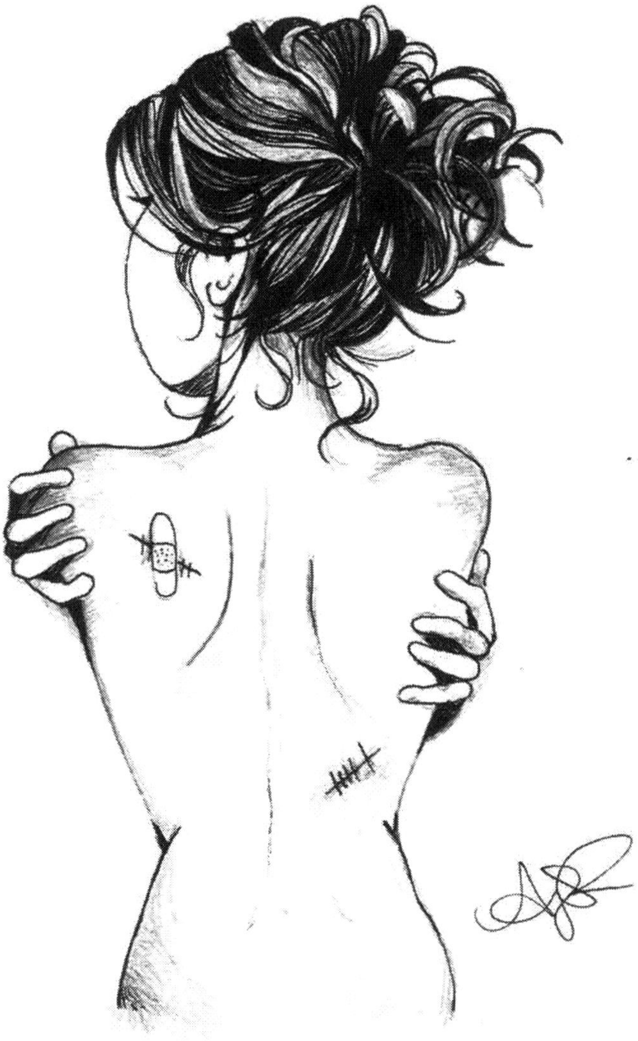

DIVORCE

A Whole Year

A whole year has gone by, and you still haven't signed the papers. A whole year has gone by because I kept thinking about you and your feelings and your reputation and what "you" could handle.

A whole year has gone by because I didn't want to disrupt and disturb your mission, or derail the course you set. I didn't want to be the cause of your failure or the reason you didn't get what you set out to accomplish.

A whole year has gone by because I forgot about myself and I thought that if I once thought about me, and what I wanted, I was being selfish and you would forever remind me of that.

A whole year has gone by because I've allowed you to be manipulative and make excuses and check out when you wanted to, and break my heart when you wanted to.

A whole year has gone by because it's always been about you and you've made sure it stays that way. And now, I'm so fucking mad at myself for being so nice and so patient and so tolerant and so helpless and so pathetic and so powerless and so weak and so stupid and so empty and so sad and so wasteful. All I have left is hyperventilation and tears.

For all my emptiness, I should be dead. There's nothing there except my eyes and my voice. I can't manage to piece together a sentence to you let alone piece it all back together in order to be more aggressive. I have it in me, but where is me? Me is away at the moment.

If I were myself, I would've never let this happen or go on this long. I'm kidnapped, waiting to be found. No, better yet, trying to escape and rejoin my dismembered self.

Narcissist can't be fixed because they don't want to be fixed. Their disorder gets them the attention they crave and allows them to use and abuse others, while still believing they are good and decent human beings.

- author unknown

The Same Person

What do you do with the energy that comes from being hurt? I suppose we all get mad and maybe it turns into rage, violence, revenge or anger. I've heard people say it's what you do with it that matters. Whatever the case, no matter what, you feel like you have to do something. I'm ambitious. I like action. I like to see things taken care of and projects finally completed. I'm results-oriented. I like when projects turn into success. I'm visual. I hate leaving loose ends and things undone. Which is probably why I am frustrated with the state of the divorce.

It has crept along for more than a year. Not because of complications, but because of inaction. And now I'm unemployed, so it's senseless to finish everything only to redo it when I do land a job. But through it all, I have learned and realized a lot. I've realized, you are the same person you were a decade ago. You are the person you've always been. You are the same person who was cheating on his girlfriend with me and telling me you weren't dating anyone. You are the person that has cheated on every girlfriend he's had. You are the same person that lied to me and could not be trusted by your then girlfriend, which is why she punched you in the face when you got home. You are the same person that's cheated on every girlfriend you've ever had, spouting the same words when you got busted, "It's not what you think." You are the same person who hasn't changed one bit but has changed so many lives around you because of the hurt you've caused. You see the hurt right in front of you, but it doesn't make you change or even apologize.

You touch the tears you made, but you are the same. You've hugged the shakes away, but you are the same. The scenario is the same for you, but you are still the same. The only thing different is the girl. You like strong women, but you can't handle them. You like passionate hearts, but you keep breaking them. You like yourself too much to change. You're the asshole. You're the liar; you're the one that's so fucked up, and you're the one who really needs therapy. Your mother fucked you up. There is something to be said about those men who didn't receive enough attention from their mothers. They always marry the best thing that ever happens to them, but because they never think they do anything wrong, they don't know how to keep them. And because narcissists are selfish, irresponsible pricks, you don't even have the decency to sincerely say, "I'm sorry." It's ironic, the same reason I cut you off for a year, 10+ years ago, is the same reason I've cut you off now. Years later, you are still the same person. This time it hurts like you've squeezed the life blood out of my heart. It didn't hurt as much before because I wasn't vested and didn't have three children. You are still the same.

The Two-Year Flatline

There was little good about the last two years. We left, but therein continued the spiral downward. God helped us because He didn't want to see me fail. The entire two years were filled with hurt and exhaustion. Finding a job, taking care of the children, dealing with him and the divorce; it all took its toll, but I couldn't stop. I couldn't rest. I couldn't pause and reflect. I had to work. I had to fight. I had to keep going. I didn't have a choice to sit one out. If I did, it was game over.

I fought for everything… money to pay a bill and when that was paid, it was on to another one. When that one was partially paid, it was yet another. I'm still ignoring much of it. I can't get to it, but they keep calling.

The two years racked up so much debt, I can't even think about it all, and yet I continue to struggle. It's still a struggle, and I can't even deal. I'm mostly numb. After you've had so many let downs, disappointments, tears, anguish, and pure shame, you start to callous and harden to it. The nerves, veins, and life; it's all flat. You can't find a vein anymore. There's too much damage.

Tenure

Devastating, crushing, disappointed… all telling words but do nothing to describe the true feeling. They all seem too cliché. They all seem empty and meaningless. They seem too surface and not deeply definitive. I wish I were a deep thinker then I could better put into words what I feel right now. My soon to be ex-husband learned he's getting tenure. Well, he is, effective a few months from now. I can't even offer a sincere congratulation. He succeeds no matter what. He doesn't even have to try, and things just work out for him. He lost his family and his wife, and it doesn't matter because he reached the ultimate achievement anyway. The mean and angry beast called "Tenure," she seeks to destroy, deconstruct, and disintegrate. It's something not many get through without loss or tears or shooting pain to the soul and heart. Many lose their soul. Many lose themselves. Many are left with only their names, and even that's questionable.

Tenure is not happy and wants to create misery. That's its mission. It's like greed. So many refuse it, but when they're in it, they can't stop themselves, it's insatiable, it's needy, and it's lovely when it all works out. But in the process…. that's the tumult… it's the process. The six years of focusing on the work is all that matters. The only thing you see is Tenure. It's calling your name. It's like the Sirens of Moby Dick; you can't look away, and when it has your attention, that's all you want. All she sees is you, and all he saw was her. She was more desirable than anything else. Everything else around you has to wait, everyone else around you has to wait and go along with it or choose another path. Not many spouses make it to the other side. Not many spouses see the purpose in the process. Not many spouses understand what the fucking point is.

I was that spouse. All the hours, all the papers, all the stress, all the strain, all the arguments, all the hate for the work, hate for the demand, all the neglect and all he wanted was her. All I saw for so many years was his back. That's what he showed me and the closer he got to her, the closer the objects in the mirror came.

His back became my favorite part. At least then he couldn't actually see me not listening about school. At least then he couldn't actually see me rolling my eyes. At least then he couldn't see me giving back to him what he gave me. The difference was he didn't care, he had already turned his back and was massaging his relationship with her. They soon became inseparable and now look at those two, they are happy, in love, in bliss, and exactly where they both wanted to be... in each other's arms. It took six years. They both got what they wanted. She has him... he has her.

Stubborn

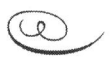

I'm stubborn, and I'm not very good at knowing when to call it quits. I keep going. Even when everything around me has burned and crumbled to the ground, I keep pushing, thinking there is a solution. I keep looking, and I keep working to make it work. I still don't know when to stop trying. I believe there is a solution to everything. What I know now, is that there's not. There's not a solution to everything if you're human. Unless you're a god or God, you can't possibly make everything work. Today, that's what I know for sure. Sometimes the solution is to stop trying.

Grant me the serenity to accept the things I cannot change, the courage to change the things I can, and the wisdom to know the difference.

- Reinhold Niebuhr

Penmanship

The shower was a bath of cleansing rain. It softened the mud caked over my thoughts and my eyes. It was so awakening. I just stood there, cupping water and splashing it over my eyes about five times. It wasn't the cupping; it was the realization that came after each cupping.

My dreams are as big as my penmanship. My Grandmother told me once, "People who write big, dream big." That was the one and only reason I needed for my big loops and letters. People, through the years, have tried to "correct" my handwriting. It's too big. It was too sloppy. It wasn't legible. He even told me once, "Your handwriting is horrible!"

This is exactly why an "ex" finally precedes his title. I hope you see the symbolism. Dreams that dwarf the dreams of others are scary and intimidating to those who believe yours will overshadow theirs. They'll never admit it. They can't. But you know your penmanship is perfect enough for those who are really reading it.

His Last Name

I have finally realized why I never felt comfortable dropping my last name and taking my husband's at the time. It wasn't necessarily about the name but about ownership. I was just enlightened by this talk. AMAZING!

http://shine.forharriet.com/2015/03/women-civil-rights-leaders-discuss.html#axzz3VdxbT7Ld

I've constantly questioned why women so quickly abandon their names and take their husbands? WHY is that? Why don't husband's take their wives' last names? Why have we given men this sense of ownership of ourselves? Who are they to command that we become theirs! We were individuals before meeting them. Why does it change when we say, "I do?" We suddenly become these people that somehow morph into one person with this man, who at times, treats you like dog shit on the bottom of his sneakers.

We are constantly fighting for them to pay attention, to listen, to care about us and care about what matters to us. We've given them our entire person, and they can't handle it. My name is who I am. My name is me, and it means a lifetime. It's the core of who we are. If we're not celebrities, we're sometimes shunned for not taking *HIS* name! Fuck that! I was never comfortable with my married last name. I compromised by keeping my maiden name and just adding his. I legally had four names. I hated the way it made me feel hearing, Mr. and Mrs. (his last name). YUCK!

If we rewind many centuries, your name was your dignity, your history, your family, and reputation. John's Son= Johnson and so on. If you were "so and so's boy or girl" it's how people defined you and formed opinions about you or what kind of person you were or the kind of person you would become. *"Oh, you're John's Son. Hum."*

What's in a name? Everything! Everything is in a name. I don't believe that not taking his last name is disgraceful, but taking his last name, for me, meant giving up who I was.

My sister easily took her husband's last name. When I asked her if she'd be keeping McHenry, she said, "I think I've been a McHenry long enough. It's time for a new name." My interpretation of that statement was more hard-hitting than what she intended. It almost took my breath away.

I remember the day at the courthouse to get our marriage license. I was so doubtful and confused about what to do about my name; whether or not I would take his, hyphenate or just double up. I felt like I was losing something if I did drop my name.

A few years later, I was at the courthouse for another matter. What I do remember about the experience was a couple conversing on the courthouse sidewalk. The guy wasn't saying much, but just standing there in the *"I'm just trying to figure out what she wants and not make her upset,"* stance. I figured they had just come from getting their marriage license, so I assumedly bid them congratulations. The girl turned to me smiled and said thank you, but then she said, "I don't know what to do about my last name and if I should take his." The look on her finance's face was a "whatever she wants to do," face because he didn't know how to help her. After I rolled my eyes and said a "Ugh, fuck him" in my head, I told her, keep your last name and just do what I did, two last names, no hyphen. She still seemed foggy. I think I just confused her more, but at least I voiced how I felt about her dilemma.

What that encounter told me was that I wasn't the only one in the world who had doubts about the subject. Although, in the midst of making the decision I did feel alone. What I knew about marriage and all that goes with it, I learned from my mother, grandmother and their friends.

BUT they learned about the tradition in the South, and that's a place where people, things, ideas, and ideals are raised stark differently than the rest of the world. I think that was part of my problem. I'm by no means a Southern woman! Although the South has nothing to do with how I feel about taking his last name, it at least gives perspective on how I see things much different than my previous generations.

I never wanted to take his last name and cringed every time I had to write it, sign it or receive mail addressed to it. I was never proud to say that name in conjunction with my first name. It never flowed or just sounded right. It never seemed to fit. It felt jagged, harsh and just wrong. I guess that sums up the marriage too.

Signing Day

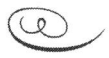

I thought I would feel liberated, relieved, and lighter when I signed the papers. Starting that morning, I kept telling myself it was a big day, but in my depth, I didn't believe that. I walked through the day anyway… just my lawyer and me.

When that moment looked at me, and the pen stood between my fingers, I did hesitate. It was a hesitant moment. It did make me stop and remember how I got to that point, and I had to remember what it was all for. I had to be sure. I wasn't sure, but I was more sure about wanting a different life without a narcissist in it.

Although the moment was a big one, I didn't feel anything after I looked at my wet signature. I made sure my penmanship was neat, careful, and legible but I didn't feel anything after I finished. I felt the same. I still felt heavy, burdened and unhappy. I thought and expected I would be happier but I just kept feeling like that wasn't all, that it wasn't final and complete. It was a huge step and a huge moment, but that wasn't all. I knew that. I felt that, but I didn't know what else there was.

One of my dear soul-mate friends asked me how I felt and I said what I thought I was supposed to say, "Great. Awesome." But it wasn't true. The truth is, I didn't know what was true. I was still lost, and so was my soul. We still hadn't run into each other. My friend congratulated and commended me. I accepted it, but the finale was still waiting for its cue.

A Narcissist will always have someone they accuse of ruining their life. It is invariably the same person the narcissist is trying to destroy.

- Narc Quotes

Vortex

I thought I was free from your grip of demise. I thought I was free from your grip of hate and darkness.

Distance doesn't prove anything when you have children. Distance is something that has a lot of space in between. There is a lot of explaining in that space, and there is a lot of confusion in that space. That space sometimes gets smaller than wider, and in that space, is love that still needs to grow, but between whom, is where the confusion lies.

Being away created its own set of complications. Poverty, depression, and sadness for everyone involved. I didn't give any thought to how you were feeling. Why the fuck would I? It was you we were getting away from. It was your dark cloud we were running away from, trying to hide in the mountains so that it didn't find us again. We hid until we thought it was safe to come out. There was never safety as long as you floated. There was always a target, and there was always energy behind the cloud. As long as you have those two, there's nothing stopping the force from doing what it does, and it doesn't even know why it does what it does; it just does.

The cloud was part of a bigger vortex that was yet to be discovered. The force and pull was nothing you could compromise with. It was something that had a mission and goal, and there's was nothing you could do to make it stop. You'll never see a mother on bended knee with her children folded in her arms pleading with the tornado to spare their lives. The tornado flips his middle finger and says, "Fuck you, get the fuck out of my way or be sucked in with the screams." It was that harsh. You were that harsh and mean and hateful. You'll never think you were, but your small cloud merged with something bigger, and yes, you are that careless.

The vortex doesn't take time to write down why or talk about its anger. It only shows you how mad it is. It rips everything it touches; it shreds souls. It's out of control. It goes, and it barrels, and it roars, and it says, "I have something to do." It doesn't necessarily have anything to prove. Anger doesn't have anything to prove. It just explodes one day until its done. When it's done, then it can settle back down. What it's left behind is its trail. What was it upset with? EVERYTHING. It can't tell you what was the one thing that set it off. It just erupts. What comes after is extreme calm. That's just how anger operates. It's not wrath because wrath has intent and wrath has a purpose and wrath is seeking to make a point. Anger just loses sanity and yells about it for a spell.

Your tantrum was the tornado.

There's a sick irony in that tantrum. It leaves behind its story, but it also leaves behind questions. What is the effect? What will it do with hearts and what will it do to the people it seemed to not give a damn about?

It's up to the people to decide their own recovery. Recovery is the hardest part because the tornado didn't care about you and how you will make sense and begin to recover. The strong stand up. The strong pull the branches from their skull and the strong patch up and keep going. The strong cry and the strong won't let anyone else see their tears. The strong take what's happened and try to work through it and push through it. But the strong are also hit with their own vulnerability, and the strong see the deeper meaning of what's happening.

Some say it's through tragedy that hearts and souls are reunited. This time it was my oldest son, who when he was nine years old named his tornado recovery charity, **ReUnite Tuscaloosa.** It was then that the vortex split open my cornea to see. This time the deeper meaning was in one letter. He capitalized the U in reunite. It's the strong who are given tough decisions to make. The universe knows they will be tasked with stress, but they will be brave enough to consider the truth. There is truth in U. There is right in U. It was me that was supposed to bring the family back together, even if you were too scared and too weak to even consider it. It was my decision to make, for the betterment of my children. Nature wasn't pulling me. Nature was aligned to let it breathe and happen naturally.

There Was a Time

There was a time that I didn't really know I was in control of my own happiness. For some reason, I thought most of it depended on someone else. That's what you talked about at the altar. The other person talked about how happy they were going to make you, and you said, "ok." You talked about it most of the months leading up to the white dress, flowers, and bullshit. He promised he would. You promised you would. Well, then life happened, and it didn't happen. He didn't make you happy. In fact, the opposite happened. He made you very unhappy. But you stayed with it. You held on, thinking it would maybe just sneak up behind you and surprise you. You kept looking over your shoulder, looking, peeking, waiting to be surprised. It never happened. The unhappiness continued. And then you realized how much it had affected all of you.

My hair was nasty, dry, brittle. My skin looked bad. No make-up could fix it. My face was tired, exhausted, and long, sadness was hanging all over it, pulling it to the floor. My body was soft, saggy. My chest, heavy with the weight of an anvil. The deep breaths made it lay heavier. There was no relief. I wasn't strong enough to lift it. It made me just slide slowly to the floor and sob. I lost control of the tears. I never knew how much water was in there behind my eyes. There were days I built a dam just for that day, just to hold the water, but there were holes everywhere. I patched them up every day, but one or two would leak out. The tears just sat there waiting on the edge of my eye-lids. They were waiting for the go-ahead, but I told them "No." It wasn't time yet. They kept telling each other, "Wait...for it." I was mad at myself for being out of control, but I couldn't cry, there was no time. I had work to do. I had little lives to take care of, and they depended on "me." I didn't want my children to see me sad, but they saw it and felt it. I had to schedule a meltdown and then re-schedule a bunch.

It almost killed me, literally. I felt close to death. Like at any minute, I was going to have a heart attack. I was afraid to take a breath. I thought it might be my last and then who would take care of my Trio? I held onto each breath, and I held it tight, so tight that squeezing made me bleed.

I had to do something. I realized I could control this. I was in charge of my own happiness, and I could do something about it. He showed me in so many ways, he couldn't and he wouldn't, and then my little girl was born. And then she started talking, and then it slapped me in the face. I told him if anyone ever treated her like I had been treated, I would kill them. It's the only time I was serious about really hurting someone I didn't know. He was silent. That was my answer and a change in my sails.

My hair is long but awesome, shiny and fluffy again that doesn't need as much product. My skin feels so much better and healthier. Make-up enhances. My eyes are brighter. I notice happiness in the little things.

Happiness is in stopping yourself at six miles when you know and feel you could keep running.

Happiness is hearing the deep, belly, gut laugh of your child.

Happiness is noticing the blue sky.

Happiness is wrapping your wet body in a big, plush, resort-style white bath sheet.

Happiness is the hint of mint in a cup of coffee.

Happiness is feeling the 60 degrees across your face and in your lungs.

Happiness is in watching your child being good and knowing that being good makes a difference.

Happiness is fitting your butt in a pair of pants you couldn't a few months ago. That's real happiness...

Happiness is in clarity of mind... body and spirit will come.

Happiness is hearing back about a job or just any response.

Happiness is realizing you don't need a lot to get by.

Happiness is knowing your children aren't worried.

Happiness is in stability.

Happiness is in getting some of your soul back. The rest is waiting for complete healing.

Happiness is in letting people do things for you.

Happiness is in letting people help you.

Happiness is in realizing you were stupid in love, but not anymore.

The Ring

I likely kept my ring longer than I should have. I didn't know how to navigate the decision to do something with it. I was caught up being nostalgic and serious about what the ring meant and what it was supposed to mean.

It's a circle. It's round. It's symbolic of the bond you have with your spouse that's never to be broken. The vows wrap the ring and your supposed happiness. My ring was a platinum band with a solitaire stone that sat in the middle of two rows of diamonds. I loved it and loved even more that it actually meant something… until it didn't.

At some point, he stopped wearing his on his finger. He wore it in on his necklace, because he "worked in the lab all day."

After a while, he stopped wearing it altogether and would give more excuses when I questioned him about why he wasn't wearing it.

I was still wearing mine proudly, but then I couldn't wait to get it off at the first sign of divorce.

I tried not to sell it, thinking I wanted to save it for my daughter, but then my thought was tainted with the reality that what it stood for was a lie and he lied to me when he gave it to me, so why would I want to pass on the toxicity to her? She deserved better, a fresh start and not someone else's broken promises.

It was time for my fresh start, and I needed the money. I held on to it until its worth was more important than its worth.

Marriage: What is it Good For?

The day I sold my wedding ring and wedding band, I cried. The tears were more truth and realization about whether or not I still believed in the act and tradition anymore. The union is hard to maintain, and that's an understatement. I guess for some people, being married is easy, but getting along every day is a choice and loving that person every day is a choice, as my priest once told me. So why would someone decide to be married? That's a question I constantly struggle with.

At least one of my friend's, married 20 years, expresses she can't even stand to hear her husband chew. HA!

Another set of friends were separated for a few weeks. I noticed he was often by himself, so I asked him how his wife was doing. It was then he told me she had gone to live with her daughter to cool off for a bit and he told her to take that yappie dog with her.

I think about these situations constantly and, with the divorce rate holding steady at 50%, I wonder what's the point of marriage!?

You no longer need marriage to have a baby. You don't need it to buy a house. You don't need it for success; you don't need it for children to feel whole and you certainly don't need it to feel complete, so what is the point!?

I remember once my brother expressing, "It's really hard!" I understood what he meant. Two people, coming together with differences in upbringing, ideas on the world, money management, and just everyday living, is hard work. What's the point of putting in that work? Not to mention, two people coming together and bringing all their past baggage with them and a narcissist who constantly abuse you and the relationship! How is anyone equipped to deal with that if you don't know the depth of the pain before the "I do."

Yes, yes. Love is healing and choosing love is what keeps it coherent and married but is it really necessary? I don't know.

What I know for sure is that for me, right now, I'm doubtful. I do want to be in love with someone, and I do want to love that person deeply, but I don't think I need marriage for it.

IF I decide to do it again, I will keep my name, keep my bank account (but he can certainly put money in it), and I will keep my life. I don't mind compromise, but I will do a better job of being my own champion.

The Bag Lady

It's taken more than three years for the love to finally finish its course. I think it's taken its last drip, but like so many things you once had, the memories of what used to be are still there. Smells, aromas, music, words, places, and food… they all are little reminders of memories we shared that were full of joy and love and laughter. What do you do with what used to be? Some say to leave the past where it is. That's not fair to just leave it behind. I feel like I need to do something with it. I don't want to bring the hurt with me, but it's not separate. It's not as easy as separating an egg. It all goes together when you've given every ounce of your life and every strand of your soul. It's all been given back to me, but I don't need it all. I want to give it to someone else. It's not that I have too much, it's just that it was supposed to be meant for someone else and he abandoned it.

I imagine it's what a homeless person feels like. Their whole life in that shopping basket being carted everywhere they go, void of finally landing and unpacking. All the memories of the life that had moments of greatness and feelings of abandonment scare you into the future. You can't avoid what's in front of you. You can't leave the effects of what used to be in the past. You may leave the thoughts and, at some point, the hurt, but the effects are worn on your sleeve, and they show through the holes of your shoes. It smells like a month of being shower-less and tired days. It shows in your mangled, matted hair. It shows in your weathered, wrinkled face. It shows on your calloused hands. It shows when you babble about nothing. It shows in the sweat-stained armpits. It shows from behind and it shows in front. All of you, what you gave, is always with you in your bag of brokenness.

It Still Hurts

Four years later and it still hurts. There are still sores that I don't realize are still open. There are times when a thought will remind me of something you did that ripped me open again and again. From slamming the Tylenol bottle on the table when I was seven months pregnant with our third child and walking out to a student meeting you didn't have to attend, telling me on the way out, "Just take these if you're in pain." I was so miserable and so sick and trying to take care two little boys and find the energy and strength to just put one foot on the floor. You were so careless, hateful, and resentful my entire pregnancy. Accusing me of getting pregnant on purpose. What the fuck is wrong with you? Who does that shit? Especially someone who is pricked by fear of her biological mother dying of an epidural overdose, a hospital is the last place I want to be. I did not enjoy pregnancy, and it was not a healthy experience, except for growing a child. You are the most hurtful person. Only thinking of yourself, once again.

It still hurts, four years later, hearing you tell me you wanted to separate when I was just a few months pregnant with our third child.

It still hurts hearing you tell me you were in love with someone else.

It still hurts, hearing you say, you just wanted to be by yourself.

One day, when real love comes to visit, I guess it won't hurt anymore, or maybe the hurt won't matter. Maybe that's just it. The hurt won't matter. But until that time... right now... It still hurts.

I'm Not Ok

I don't show it, and everyone thinks that I'm ok. Everyone thinks that I've moved on and, because I'm usually smiling or laughing, that I'm ok. I'm not honest when people ask how I'm doing. I don't think they really want to know. I feel like it's a courtesy question. Nevertheless, I tell them I'm doing fine.

I'm not. I'm still hurting, and I cry when I read about how hurt I am. I don't know what to do with my feelings and emotions. Therapy is too trite. I can't do that. It's totally expected, and it's what everyone does when something tragic has happened. *GOD, I don't want to talk about it with someone I'm paying to listen!* FUCK!!! What interest do they have in you when that's the shit they hear all day? I'm not doing that. I'm sure they can help but, ugh! I don't have time to keep going back. So, I sit and hold it together every day and just live with it.

Letting Go

My mind has been telling me to write this chapter for quite a while. I didn't know where to start because it's a process, much like the topic of this chapter is a process.

Letting go is a process. I hate that phrase because it's basic and regular. Having said that, letting go is not something that you can actually do by the next day. It takes hours, minutes, days, weekends, months, years, and then what seems like a lifetime.

When you've committed to something like marriage and have given your soul to making it work, and when it doesn't work, it breaks you and your soul into a thousand pieces. If you're a strong woman, you keep trying to make it work. If you're stubborn and you refuse to throw in the towel, you keep trying to make it work until you realize, you're the only one trying.

In that case, it's not going to work, and you have to walk away.

I don't know, though, if you necessarily let go in that moment of realization. The investment happened over a period of time, so I'd say it will take that long to completely let go.

It's been six years since my divorce and, over time, I've let pieces go a little at a time. Some things were easy… living together, parenting together (that never really happened, so that was painless), hanging out together, family time, and so many other things.

What was more difficult to let go of was the idea of us, the idea of being married, the commitment of marriage, and the idea of what I wanted my family to be. My parents were married for more than 40 years before my

Mom passed this year. I've grown up in a two-parent household, and my parents had each other's back ALWAYS! My Dad would pounce if we for one instance disrespected my mother in any way. They were in-sync, and there was nothing we could do that would get past one of them. Eventually, one would tell the other. It was usually my Mom telling my Dad when he came home from work (always a family joke).

That's what I wanted for my children and my life. My Dad is a definite family man who loves holidays, family time, socializing and overall loves people. Most of all, he loves his children immensely and is passionate about being a close-knit family. He loves family and loves the idea of a bonded family. That's what I wanted for my children. Family is incredibly important to me, and when I realized my children weren't going to have that, it added to my brokenness and feeling of failure. I was so disappointed that I couldn't do better, that I couldn't fight harder, and that I had to let go of those ideas because they were no longer my reality and no longer my truth. That is gut-wrenchingly devastating!

I think the fact that I held on to those facades is what kept me in the marriage about five years too long. I kept thinking that what was important to me would also be important to him, and that somehow if he didn't see it as important for himself, he would want that because we had children. The fact is, the children had nothing to do with his narcissism. He was in himself, in his own world, that only involved him and therefore, letting go of wanting to be paid attention to and supported and given a hand every once in a while, was what I had to let go of next.

Letting go of hope, our future together, growing old together, raising children in one household and sharing love for all the things that we had in common were all things I had to let go of.

That's a lot of shit! If you commit wholeheartedly, with your entire being, then you, when you said, "I do," let go of much of yourself too. I let go of the hope that he could take care of me and listen to me and want to be with me.

Letting go also means that all the dreams that you shared together are now singled out. They're individual. You no longer have dreams together. Either you take them or he takes them, or you just take what you want and leave the rest. Of all the things you let go of though, you gain a little bit of freedom each time.

Don't Be Mad

I did everything… taking care of the children, making sure the bills were paid, tending to every matter under the sun and on and on and on and on. You know the scenario. I felt frustrated and upset that I wasn't getting more help. I would constantly ask for it only to be rejected or lied to. The constant disappointment led to resentment. The resentment led to bitterness which led to a hardened heart. A hardened heart led to an increased feeling of being burdened and a constant wonderment about why I needed him and why I was still hanging on to something where hope had expired.

I was incredibly angry for so long because I had to be the one to make a plan and the decisions constantly fell on my shoulders. I was so mad about that feeling affecting my inner peace. I had none. I felt like my face was constantly wrinkled because I was always thinking and always upset about having to be the one to do the thinking and managing.

But it suddenly occurred to me, don't be mad about having to do everything. Be empowered by knowing you can do everything. It's when you're forced into a situation that you realize what your body, soul, mind, and spirit are capable of. Maybe it's not something you trained for, and it's certainly not what you intended for your life when you became partners, but life doesn't prepare you for itself. You learn about it as you keep living and, in learning, you discover what you're made of. How you feel, how you go about life, how you respond, and how you adjust your view on the situation comes down to perspective. When you change your thinking, you realize that being mad about your situation only makes you crazy. Instead, be thankful that you are capable of handling the world! You're a bad ass!

Love's Lost

It's a confusing thing when you find yourself wondering what to do with the all love that's now been handed back to you. It's like being handed a baby for too long. You have no idea how long you should hold it, when to give it back to its owner, pass it to someone else or cradle it for a while until you hush the crying.

It's like you grow extra body parts to accommodate the extra "being in love" with someone and when it's over, the limbs just dangle, turn grey or white from the blood loss. Dying takes time. In the meantime, you're stuck with the bucket.

It's so sad and painful as you figure out how to do a do-over. It takes a while to completely shelve the love you had for that person back in your heart. One signature on divorce papers doesn't do anything or cut off the love. It's still there in your hands, especially if you never held any if it back. You can't put the gum back in the dam hole. You just have to wait for it to run out.

I Want to Hate You

I want to hate you for all the ways you hate yourself.

I want to hate you for all of your inadequacies.

I want to hate you for the situation you put me in.

I want to hate you because I'm still struggling.

I want to hate you because you leave everything up to me and you get to pick and choose what you want to do and how you want to be involved.

I want to hate you for expecting me to bend over and touch my toes so you can fuck me in the ass.

I want to hate you for expecting me to be stupid.

I want to hate you for expecting me to always think of a plan.

I want to hate you because you only do the bare minimum and even that was forced upon you.

I want to hate you because you have to be forced to be a basic dad.

I want to hate you because even your basic doesn't measure up to the standard of basic.

I want to hate you because you're basic.

I want to hate you because you're sloppy and a drunk and don't care about anything, especially not your children.

I want to hate you because you get to be mediocre and you're ok with that.

I want to hate you because your only desire for motivation and zeal is how it will benefit you.

I want to hate you for expecting me to be silent.

I want to hate you for expecting me not to fight.

I want to hate you for expecting me not to be someone other than I am.

I want to hate you for hoping I would be weak.

I want to hate you for hoping I would break and stay broken.

I want to hate you for turning your back on my tears and pain.

I want to hate you for being surprised when I rise up and speak out and fight back.

I want to hate you for being unsupportive.

I want to hate you for being jealous.

I want to hate you for not being happy when I succeed.

I want to hate your for teaching my children it's ok to be disrespectful to their mother.

I want to hate you for disrespecting the mother of your children.

I want to hate you for disrespecting the mother of your children.

I want to hate you for disrespecting the mother of your children.

I want to hate you for thinking I'm the bitch of your problems.

I want to hate you because your mother didn't teach you how to respect women.

I want to hate you because your dad was ok with your mother not teaching you to respect and cherish women and he didn't teach you to do better.

I want to hate you because our children experience your narcissism and selfishness first-hand.

I want to hate you because that's what breaks my heart the most.

I want to hate you because you are a piece of shit.

I want to hate you because I couldn't accept who you were and I wanted and hoped you were different and decent.

I want to hate you because you put on a show in front of others.

I want to hate you because you lie and think people don't see you.

I want to hate you because you've lied so much that to you, it's the truth.

I want to hate you for thinking that taking responsibility is placing blame and putting your responsibility on others.

I want to hate you for squelching my power and thinking the fire was permanently distinguished.

I want to hate you for leaving me to die.

I want to hate you because you suck.

But I'm not a hateful person, and I can't bring myself to hate. My soul's love is joyous, filled with the grace of God and doesn't have room for hate. I want to hate you, but I can't because you're miserable and I'm not.

Mostly, I want to hate you because…. You don't know any better.

Narcissists don't co-parent, they counter-parent. They don't care about the collateral emotional damage done to the children, as long as it hurts you.

- Whisper

Grieving Children

What I learned last night is that my oldest son is more than smart, he is a divine creature whom God gave his own wisdom to. His name is Emmanuel, which means God with us. God was never more present in his room last night.

Last night, the house was fighting and full of tension, dissension, and stress. I had no idea why. Everyone was yelling, and then I let out the ultimate momma bear yell over everyone else to calm things down. That didn't really help.

Emmanuel and I were going back and forth about Legos, and it was such a stupid argument. Then, when I realized I was arguing with my 13-year-old, I got even more upset that he was bold enough to go toe-to-toe with me, expressing himself in a way I thought later was disrespectful. I finally figured I needed to shut it down, but it was going nowhere and frankly, I was so tired of having yet another argument about Legos. So, I yelled at him, told him his attitude was atrocious, and threatened him with talking to my Dad about it (which scares them into submission).

Then it was time for everyone to go to bed. Everything was just heavy. My middle son was having a meltdown about his cracked Lego guy. My daughter was upset, and Emmanuel was just plain mad.

Then it all came out. When I asked Emmanuel what he was upset about, he began to tell me that when me and his dad fight, it causes incredible pressure, discomfort, and anxiety in his soul. He hates it. It makes him feel hopeless, and he just wants to go back to when we were all a family and living together. That's the hardest part of divorce, trying to give your children a sense of hope in a situation that will never be the same. They just want it to be the same, but it will never be, and that's the thought and reality that changes their world, for better or worse.

They don't care whether or not the situation was good or bad when their parents were married; they just want stability, hope, and peace. They don't understand that either parent could not continue to live under the conditions of a narcissistic, bad marriage and you had to save yourself and your children. They don't yet understand that the divorce was part "rescue mission."

What they do always know and understand, then and now, is that something isn't right. Whether or not parents argue in front of their children, they always still know and subconsciously know their parents are drifting apart and that scares them. I haven't read divorce books; I haven't gone the route of voluntary therapy either. I can't afford it, and really, I don't have time.

I don't think putting myself or my children in a situation where they are given an hour at a time and told they can talk about what they want is always helpful. I don't know they will be comfortable opening to a stranger, but I could be completely wrong. I have friends who believe whole-heartedly in therapy. I'm not so sure about it. The sessions I have been a part of have not been helpful. We went the marriage counseling route, and things got worse. The counselor told us we should probably get divorced. He didn't have enough information, and my ex was not being open and honest. I do know there was no way we could stay together. I just didn't expect that the Christian marriage counselor would suggest divorce. I thought his job was to help us work things out. That was a shock.

Later, I was ordered to therapy by the courts when my ex and I were fighting again. That was an expensive disaster. Not only was the counselor a bad mediator but she placated and bad-mouthed each of us behind the other's back. She let us fight and lose focus of why we were there in the first place. After two-sessions, I stopped going. There was no point in continuing to spend money on something that had no positive outcome. I haven't had good experiences in counseling and therapy, so I don't know that it's for me and my family.

What I do know is that my children are wise and intuitive beyond belief. Listening to them share what's on their hearts and in their brains is truly astonishing. What I know for sure is that they will always know their voice, opinions, and thoughts mean something in our home. They are always free to tell me what they think about anything. There is a limit to how far they can go, especially if they are bordering disrespect, but their feelings always matter, and their voice always matters to me.

It's important to me because growing up was starkly opposite. My voice, thoughts, and opinions didn't matter to my parents. I was not given freedom and confidence in that space. We didn't speak out because that wasn't allowed. My parents were old-school.

That night turned into a lot of shed tears. My children's hearts are hurting. I wanted to tell them the truth, but I also wanted them to know I was on their side and understood what they were feeling.

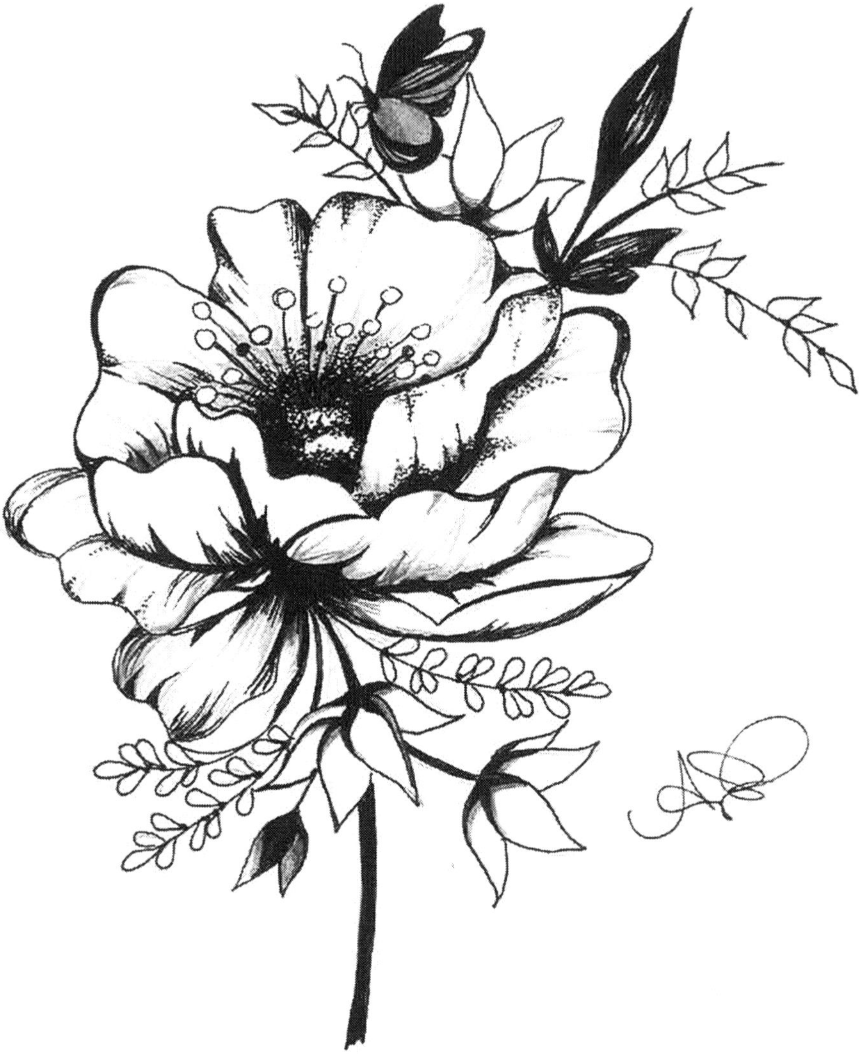

Part Two
Lessons Learned

The Sad Rich Girl

We know the narcissist without ever meeting them in person. She wears a heavy diamond. She drives a luxury SUV. She smiles constantly, and it looks genuine. She seems full of joy and full of money. She can spend hundreds of dollars on a whim, but even the girls with money, a renovated bungalow, a rich husband in an exclusive neighborhood, are sad. We all know this girl. This girl who thought she'd be happy with the guy that all the girls wanted but then she got him with her list of ultimatums, and when he didn't change, she didn't want him because he wanted her existence. He took her existence, and her dignity and her self-worth and her life and she spends her stresses thinking of how she's going to ask for a little bit of it back every day.

Some days she talks herself out of asking because the night before he yelled at her about something else and with that mental beating, he snatched the crumb of confidence she worked up. Now she has to wait about three days before she tries again. Those next three days she loses herself again and again and tells herself it was her fault and she should've been better, done better, and anticipated that he was going to flip out.

She lives in his existence. She makes decisions based on how he feels and how she expects he will feel. He's the narcissist which means he's predictable, most of them time. That's the only easy part of the relationship. She knows what he'll do, so she decides not to do, not to say, not to act, not to react, not to think, not to feel, not to breathe too hard, not to walk with confidence, but rather timidly in his existence.

The only thing she decides to do is what she thinks he wants her to do. The only other thing she decides to do is what will keep him from treating her like shit, and then she decides that it's easier just to keep waiting, remain quiet and sad, sitting on a pile of his money.

Anger

I've spent so much time and energy being angry. I've been angry at what my ex has not done for the sake of my children. I've been angry about what he's done to me. I've been angry about his being selfish. I've been angry about things that he can't change- that's what I've been most angry about. I've been angry about my inability to accept the things I can not change. I've been angry about my inability to accept him for who he really is.

Maya Angelou said it best, "When someone shows you who they are, believe them." I could not accept that. I wanted better for my children. I wanted better for their life. I was angry because he couldn't provide that. He couldn't be that, and that made me angry.

"How could he be that person?" was a thought I constantly repeated. How could a person who has children do... *fill in the blank*. Because narcissists don't know how to be better. They don't know how to not think about themselves. They don't know how to do what's best for the children. They only know how to do what's best for them, and they only know how to do what's going to hurt you the most.

It wasn't that I thought I could change him. Actually, yes. I thought I could change his ways, but I also thought his changing would be innate and would come naturally once he had children. I thought he would want to do things that would be better for the children, but narcissists can only think about themselves, and it doesn't matter if they have children. That's what's most angering!

Bad Mom

One of the most difficult realities of dealing with a narcissist ex-husband is that nothing you do is right. They will constantly tell the children you're to be blamed for ridiculous things and will constantly try to discredit you as a parent and discredit your parenting. They won't support your discipline or your structure for the children. They will tell the children lies about you and they will talk badly about you to the children. The psychological abuse to the children is terribly damaging. The worst part is that they will tell the children how wrong your rules and principles are and that when they're with him, they can do whatever Mom has not allowed in her home. It's psychologically and emotionally injurious to the children, and it's frustratingly confusing. They don't know who to believe. They don't know what is truth, and they will use that information to constantly challenge you, saying things like, "Well, at Daddy's house…."

It makes me so stressed because I want to scream expletives, but I have to hold my tongue with hot tongs until I can bitch with my girlfriends and my sister.

I pray every day that God will give each of my children discernment and intuition. I believe in my heart that God opens their eyes and hearts to the truth. Feel safe in knowing that they see the situation for what it is. Over time, you won't need to explain anything to them… they already know. Whether or not they accept the truth is something they'll need to come to on their own terms.

When divorcing a narcissist, prepare for the rage.

- Huffington Post

Beware: They Will Unravel

Here's your warning, when you start to create boundaries, when you move away, when you put any distance between yourselves, the narcissist will begin to unravel.

In your head, it may seem easier just to stay and endure, but you can't. Staying is horrific. But, it's likely that moving away from it all will be horrific too, especially if you have children together. However, with clarity, you will learn to handle it differently.

As I mentioned in a previous chapter, narcissists despise losing control of a situation. Their power and energy come from manipulation and if they can't manipulate a situation, they turn their energy and attention to finding another way to come after you. They will try to turn your children against you and assassinate your character. They'll try and find people who would gladly help them, but the spirits of those groupies are just as broken.

It's something you definitely should be mentally, spiritually, and physically prepared for. They will continue to unravel and they will continue to try and cause you mental and emotional harm.

My ex-husband is still unraveling, and we've been divorced seven years at this point. He's so consumed with anger that I never know what he'll say or do. He's unfiltered, and he's even stooped so low as to call me a 'fucking idiot' to my face one day at weekend drop-off. I am the mother of his children. His disrespect and unraveling are so severe; he couldn't hold his tongue. It shocked my system, as I think it would anyone. I never expected it, but I should have. It wasn't the first time he yelled at me or called me a horrible name, but it had been a while, so I wasn't prepared in that moment.

Nevertheless, it still felt like he spat in my face. It knocked the wind out of me and it stunned me. He spoke the words with such vile hatred; he may as well have shot me at point blank range or stabbed me 70 times. The children being present made it worse because I couldn't do anything. I couldn't fight back. I couldn't hit him. I couldn't back over him with my car (not that I would have but you know what I mean- I did think about it). They drive you to the brink of insanity. He said it and immediately turned and walked away because he's weak. The smartest thing I could do was to just get in my car and drive off. That upset me because I wanted to lose it, but I couldn't do anything in front of my children, and he knew that. He knew exactly what he was doing. Ultimate manipulation!

They will unravel so let them. Let them be a fool. Let them show who they really are and try and keep your involvement in it to a minimum. Let them light their own fires. Just be sure to back away from the fray. It will be difficult to control your responses and your emotions, but it will be in your best interest to let them unravel alone.

When you are ready to leave, also remember to be ready and guard your heart and soul because just like winter came in *Game of Thrones*, the unraveling is coming too.

You're a Fucking Idiot

I wish I could say it was an isolated incident, but it wasn't. He has used such vile, putrid language before and yes- just like the times before- to my face.

What kind of human being is so angry, so mean, so hateful, so spiteful that they could say that to someone who bore their children? They don't care about that. They don't care about anything. They want you to feel how they do, and of course, how they feel inside is your fault. You caused their anger; you caused them to treat you the way that they do. You forced their hand, and so they had to spout off such hatred because, after all, if you hadn't done that thing that upset them, they would've never called you a fucking idiot.

Isn't it amazing that someone actually raised a human being like that and continues to enable them into adulthood? This person has a mother who didn't teach human decency and respect. Isn't it amazing that this person's mother did not teach him to respect women? Isn't it amazing to know that if you did tell that person's mother what their child said to you, you know in your heart they would believe you caused their child to react that way? Their mother would probably say something like, "Everyone says things like that to each other," or "What did you say to him before he called you that?" or "My child would never say anything like that!" or the ultimate, "You probably deserved it." That person's mother would never believe you and more importantly, believe that their precious adult-child did anything wrong; and that's why, ladies and gentleman, you get called a "Fucking Idiot."

But this is the evolution of a narcissist. Their disorder blooms from their relationship with their mother. What I've learned is that narcissists have a distorted mother/child relationship. Their mothers idolize them, never believing that their children do anything wrong, which results in them thwarting responsibility for any of their actions, especially the actions that cause others harm.

My ex got arrested for drunk driving and charged with a DWI. His mother told him the breathalyzer reading of being twice over the legal limit was false. It wasn't the alcohol that elevated his blood alcohol level according to her; it was the chemicals he was working with in the lab that infiltrated his blood stream and did him in.

He dropped our infant. "everyone drops their baby," she said.

On another occasion, he was wobbling, crashing into walls, drunk again. He mentions to his mother, he only had a few beers and he knows that they [his parents] think he's an alcoholic. "You're not an alcoholic," she tells him.

The responses became commonplace leaving you in further disbelief. Enablers often tell the narcissists that whatever has happened is someone else's fault and not theirs.

Now, do you want to know what led him to call me a "fucking idiot?" Well, it's more than just one reason, but on this particular occasion, he was upset at my discipline methods. My oldest son got his phone taken away for disobedience. His father suggested I take something else away because "the iPhone 5 is such a crucial part of a 15-year-old's education and he really needs it to get his work done."

Oh yes, I did read that article which cited scientific proof that scores of kids are failing school because their parents are confiscating their digital devices. "Would you take away his pens and pencils?" he says.

I was called a fucking idiot because I'm trying to teach my children the importance of following instructions and the consequences you face when you don't. His father believes I'm a fucking idiot for doing so.

Truth

To be disrespected is the ultimate degradation, but to be devalued as a human being is the lowest cancellation of human worth there is. It's an amazing experience when you're at the mercy of someone else's narcissistic insecurities. Their insecurities arrest them in fear. That fear keeps them from looking inward, and the ignorance keeps a hold of your soul. As long as you stay, your soul is theirs. They can't let go because that would mean the truth will break through much faster, but if they hold your soul and you at bay, then truth has to fight for its freedom.

Truth is an Amazonian Warrior who can't be destroyed. She never takes a break. She never rests. She's always fighting to be seen. She is the only thing that never gives up, but is patient with the process. Truth is the one thing that will always show up. You can have faith in it. You can trust it. You can be certain of it, and you can count on it. It can take years to come to your aid, but believe; it's on the way. It's always on your side. This Amazon Warrior fights every day for you. She is victorious, and she is invincible. She can take fire, she can take bullets, she can take punches, hot prods, and even burial, but her life is immortal.

She gravitates toward light. The darkness blankets her, but it's only temporary. She plays dead, but she's not. She rolls over but not because she's given up. She was waiting for the right time because timing is everything to make the ultimate, lasting impact. Truth never hides, is never afraid and only knows one way to be.

When believers understand her and give her faith, it strengthens her resolve. It's just a matter of time before she appears. You never have to worry about whether or not someone will know the truth of the situation or the narcissist. She will make sure of it!

Be **confident** in knowing you know the truth and she knows you!

Within Reason

It's impossible to reason with a narcissist because they are not reasonable thinkers. Something you think is simple and doesn't require much energy, will become an issue, a big deal, and will likely turn into an argument.

Yes, you are the reasonable thinker. Things that you think are easy should be easy to agree on, and shouldn't take much time to sort out, but things will become the exact opposite, and you'll be baffled that it suddenly turned into a thing. To you, it's senseless that it's now a thing and you'll walk around stressed out because in your mind, it was never a big deal and it wasn't supposed to turn into one.

Once you learn to accept that, no, you can't ask them just to go pick up your child from school because you're tied up for a bit longer, things will be less stressful for you. It seems easy, right, that they would understand your dilemma and would just step in, be the cooperative co-parent and help you out for the sake of your child. It's not that easy. They are very uncooperative. They don't co-parent, they anti-parent if it's something *you* need from them for the sake of your children. They don't think about what's best for you or the child. Their only motivation is them and what matters to them. Narcissists need to know if there's something in it for them.

My friend Taylor (we'll change her name for privacy sake) thought she could call her ex, and ask him if he would take their daughter to lunch while she was in a meeting. After all, they both work at a university and in the summer, their schedules are lighter. They were in the middle of yet another trip to court where he was asking the judge for more time; he wanted to spend more time with their daughter. My friend, the reasonable thinker, thought he would say, "Yes, absolutely, I'd love to spend an extra hour with my daughter, especially since I'm petitioning the courts for more time. I'm not busy this afternoon, and it will be great!" Seems easy and reasonable, right? Not so much! It turned into a big deal. He couldn't understand the request and was too busy. He had other things going on in the afternoon, blah, blah, blah. Taylor knew her ex wasn't busy because they had already discussed his afternoon. It's the only reason she asked him if he wanted to maybe have lunch with their daughter but no, it didn't go well.

Once you accept that their way of thinking is distorted and that you cannot reason with a narcissist, you will be much happier and less stressed. Your conversations will become limited, and you'll have to make more decisions on your own when it comes to the children. You'll think twice about wanting to reach out to them about things that seem basic to you. Basic to you is outrageous to them.

Weak

Narcissists are weak people with low self-esteem. Their entire existence is a facade. They suffer from an inflated ego to make you think they are someone that they are not. They love attention, and they love to put on a show. They love grandeur; they love their name being called on the big screen. They love to see themselves. They love the stage; they love theatrics. They also love to call attention to themselves and their fake accomplishments. They love recognition and compliments. If it's not about them, they somehow manipulate the situation, so it eventually becomes about them.

I now understand why birthday parties, Christmas and any event that brought attention to someone else, even our children, would be a problem and would cause him to behave differently.

I now understand why he had such a problem when my family visited. My family and I are close. We love being together. We love hanging out, and we love to laugh and have a good time. He hated that because my attention would be elsewhere, not on him. He would constantly disappear when they came to visit, or he would try his best to alienate me from them. I was constantly interrupted on phone calls with any of my family members, even my Grandmother. He would pretend he had to tell me something or show me something that couldn't wait. It was like interacting with a 2-year old. His weak and low self-esteem couldn't handle the attention not being on him for even two minutes. He was constantly trying to pull me away and ultimately separate me from my loved ones so he'd be the ONLY important person in my life.

I now understand how he and I slowly drifted apart after each of my children were born. Most of my attention went to them and that, he couldn't handle. He became resentful, and he didn't help me with them. I did everything! There was no such thing as taking turns with over-night feedings, diaper changes, dropping off at school and EVERYTHING that babies and children require. When I asked for help, I got a verbal lashing! He was resentful and accused me of all kinds of crazy things, and he generally became more and more neglectful.

Narcissists lie and say the most egregious and outrageous things. It doesn't matter to them that none of it is true. What matters is your believing it. They believe their lies, but I'm not sure if they really know they're lying. They lie so often, it's second nature, and it's what their mouth usually spouts.

They are constantly projecting. They want to you believe that they are the most amazing people in the world. They can do no wrong, and when you try and call them out on something, they tell you it's you that's doing what you've accused them of.

While they love attention, they love positive attention. Negative attention only makes them angry, and their weak core and weak nature can't handle it. Rather than look inwardly and accept what is true about themselves, they will ignore what's within and not accept what they've done to offend you. Instead, they try and flip the situation, so you appear to be the crazy one.

It's an insane psychotic cycle that will make you feel wacky and out of your mind. Believe me; it's not you. It's them. They are master manipulators and master liars. Their inflated egos and overall pompous nature is over compensation and an attempt to hide their weakness and low self-esteem. They believe they're always right and it's you that they think needs to change, not them. They don't believe they've done anything wrong, so it's best not to tell them. The best way to shut down a narcissist is to tell them, "You're right" and move on. You won't change them. They are incapable of understanding and seeing the need to change. You won't be able to penetrate them. What you can do though, is stand your ground, create boundaries and stick to that. They will be angry, and they will fly off the handle, they will write you horrible emails and hurtful texts messages. Try not to take it personally. Step away from it and see it as their weakness. Don't engage with a narcissist. The argument is not worth the mental strain and stress it will cause you. Your energy is better spent on you. For strong people like us, this is one of the hardest things in life to do because you want them to also see things from your perspective and you want them to understand your hurt, your pain, your position on something, but frankly, they can't, and they don't want to. They won't believe they've caused you any pain or hurt. They won't apologize.

A conversation that eventually becomes an argument with a narcissist will leave you more angry and frustrated. Don't engage. Rather, keep a cool head, smile, and tell them, they're right. They'll be speechless.

Sometimes You have to Lose the Battle to Win the War

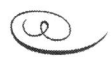

I recently told my Dad that I was sorry for what I may have done during my marriage that offended him and my Mom. "I wasn't myself then," I apologized. With sincere grace and pure love, my Dad let me know he understood and knew I was having a hard time. He and my Mom, now passed away, forgave me a long time ago. My parents knew things weren't right and they saw how I was being treated. They saw first-hand my ex-husband's drunkenness. They saw first-hand his marital neglect. They repeatedly witnessed his alcoholism and narcissistic abuse.

Although they knew I wasn't being physically abused, they knew the mental and psychological turmoil was changing and breaking me. But they didn't know if or how they should step in- they didn't want to make things worse by causing dissension. I didn't know how to tell them that it was already horrible and they couldn't do anything to make it any worse. Our minds were connected. They felt it.

I spent several years of my marriage being angry at them for things my ex-husband brought to my attention about them. He pointed out anything negative, from their parenting style to ways they treated us siblings differently, to practically anything that would make them look bad. There was constant tension when my parents visited, and I hated how that felt. My Dad didn't like my choice in a husband from the beginning, but my Dad tried his best to like my ex-husband because he knew I loved him. My ex-husband was constantly challenging my Dad on everything- the Bible, doctrine, science, the universe, Christianity and on and on. He would constantly tell me how wrong my Dad was about everything and that he didn't know much about anything. Now that I look back, I realize it made my ex happy to see me fighting with and yelling at my parents. It felt like he was internally giddy when I argued with them and/or my siblings about petty things. I was engulfed in the whirlwind of tension and wanted to make our marriage work, but my ex tried to turn me against everyone that I loved, which is another narcissistic tactic.

He worked tirelessly to drive a wedge between my parents and me, and he did. I would go long bouts without talking to my parents, and that was unusual because we are a close family and my Dad and me, in particular, have always been close..... but that was the problem.

Narcissists want to be your number one focus and your only priority. Although they are unwilling to give you the same priority, they demand it from you in every way they can. You don't always see it because it's rarely tangible.

My parents could see I wasn't happy. They did their best to support me, and I know they prayed for me and my children.

Now that my distress beacon is flickering less, I can see the bigger picture. After the divorce, my Dad wanted to help me reduce the stress of dealing with my ex. He constantly advised me to focus on the bigger picture and not get caught up in the small little battles. "Sometimes you have to lose the battle to win the war, and this is a war," he advised me.

His heavy advice was loaded with wisdom. What he meant was, don't get into a shouting match or a back and forth about the small stuff, it only makes you more stressed. Don't fight about the children returning home on Sunday without showering all weekend and still wearing Friday's school clothes, just continue teaching them about the importance of taking responsibility for their own hygiene, since their father won't.

"Don't pick a fight about what he lets the children do at his house. Don't pick a fight about how much time they spend in front of a screen. Talk to your children about self-discipline," my Dad cautioned.

"Walk away from volatile situations and don't have a conversation with him. You have nothing to discuss with him. Tell him to talk to your lawyer. Why are you engaging him? Stop doing that!" he said emphatically.

"Your ex doesn't care what you want to for the sake of your children. He knows how to get to you, and that's his focus. He wants to disrupt and crumble every good thing you've put in place because you've done an incredible job with your children and he can't handle that."

I was so caught up in the storm that everything made me upset. I was blowing up on the inside every other weekend.

What I realize now is that I was prepping myself to be upset because I had expectations of my ex. I expected him to do his job. I expected my children would be returned in good condition and when they weren't, I lost it. My children could feel the tension, and they could feel me. My being upset only made them feel like I was always upset with their dad. Although I was, I needed to get a better grip and not let them see that from me. I'm not that great at hiding my feelings. Padding myself with anger further delayed my arrival at internal peace.

I had to let go of my expectations and, believe me, that was not easy. It behooves me to actually accept that I can have no expectations of another human being that I share children with. It's a crazy thought, but it's a necessary thought when dealing with a narcissist. Your only expectation of them is that they are a narcissist who will behave as such. Nine times out of 10, their behavior will not be in the best interest of your children, and it's best if you accept that statistic quickly.

My Dad is incredibly wise and has great foresight. Every piece of advice he offers is laced with a Bible lesson. It took me a while to hear what he said to me. I just wasn't trying to hear it because it didn't feel like my ex's neglect was small. I take the well-being of my children very seriously. I'm a mama bear, and I pounce! I wanted to be mad, and I wanted to bitch about it more. I figuratively beat my head against the wall until I bled, but I finally came around and visualized my Dad's words.

Losing the battle for the sake of winning the war is an awakening metaphor. You can't spend your energy fighting little battles that continue to interrupt your clarity. Your focus should be on the war- the war to win yourself back and to protect your children.

When you can tell your story, and it doesn't make you cry, that's when you know you've healed.

- Quotling

Stay Above the Fray

❝ Stay above the fray" is what I tell myself daily and every time I get an email or text from my ex-husband. Whenever I see his name in my inbox, I get anxious and nervous. I get heartburn and hot flash. The emotions are occurring less now though. After my Mom passed, I started to give care less about the bullshit and all of it from him was straight bullshit, so I didn't care anymore about anything he tried to derail me with and believe me, he threw out a lot of spikes.

Narcissists love to fight. It's all they have when you leave. The leaving could be physical first, then mental, and then psychological. The order has no preference or partiality. The fact is that leaving, in whatever way you've left, leaves them void, so their only choice is to engage and continue being abusive because they know no other way of being. The only way for them to stay empowered is to just fight... about literally ANYTHING!

They want you to react. They want you to respond and engage. They want you to get upset. They want you to scream back or return the insult. That's how they remain empowered and in control. But when you can get to the point of not caring and letting it all roll off your back, then you have deflated their bloated disorder. Although you may be poking their eyes out with your middle fingers in our imagination, simply smile or politely giggle at their toddler tantrum... in that instant, you've disrupted and stolen their power.

When they feel threatened, they attack. Leaving is a threat to them. Even if you've left physically, they will still try and stay engaged. They will still call, and when they come visit the children, things may go well for some of the visits, but things may explode during others. They will find something that you've done incorrectly that you will certainly be criticized for, but stay above the fray.

Staying above the fray is this: not taking anything they say or do personally. Don't be offended that they don't remember the truth. They don't want to remember the truth. The truth doesn't exist or matter to them. The truth is something for other people, not for them. Staying above the fray is not letting yourself get twisted and mixed up in their sick disorder. Just agree with them. Your way of saying "fuck you" should be simply saying, "You're right." That shuts them down instantly. It may kill you on the inside to say those two words, "You're right," but remembering to not take it personally will be your saving grace… keeping your personal peace and your sanity.

All of the discrepancies they seem to have a problem with are facades. They find things to ignite a fight about. They will bring up things that happened years ago that you've since forgotten about. They will be appalled that you don't remember because it was such a BIG issue then. You will question your conscience about why they're even bringing it up. While it may have been something you constantly tussled about then, it doesn't really matter anymore when you're divorced, and the fact that they want to fight about it is another clue of their narcissism.

Right now, our relationship is extremely contentious. Anything I do, my ex-husband sees as a threat to himself. Narcissists only think about themselves, and they constantly feel victimized. They will needlessly drag you back to court as much as they can. It will be expensive and it will be frustrating that lawyers and judges will take on and hear these bogus cases. You will wish the law would see them as frivolous and dismiss the nonsense but I now believe that everyone is in it to make money. Courts want to see you fighting. It's another way they make money and I'm cynical to it all.

On one of my ex-husband's visitation weekends, my daughter had a piano recital. She was so worried that her unreliable Dad wouldn't take her that she begged and pleaded with me all week to stay home with me to ensure she would get to her recital on-time and that she would have time to prepare beforehand. After feeling sick about it and getting over being scared of what he'd do, I obliged and kept her home. Instead of thinking about our daughter and her scared concern, he got so angry with me, he called the cops and claimed that I was keeping my daughter just to keep her away from him. Narcissists also love to cause a scene, bringing attention to themselves. He was so intent on getting back at me, because he felt threatened and victimized, that he purposely made sure my oldest son saw and was present for the entire exchange between him and the police. The dramatic scene happened outside my middle son's school during a school dance. If he had any care or concern for the well-being of our children, he wouldn't have been upset at all, and he certainly wouldn't have called the police in front of our son, just to cause a scene and make a point.

Staying above the fray meant that I could not react negatively to this. I didn't get caught up in the ludicrousness of his actions. I know there's nothing the police can do and they certainly weren't going to hop in their units and chase me down to the street. When I was caught up in the fray, I would've been scared, nervous, and practically throwing up with fear when he whipped his phone out and dialed 911. Because I vowed to stay above the fray, I calmly got in my car, told him "Whatever" and slowly drove away with my daughter in the car.

When you can take just a couple minutes to think rationally and not let the narcissist scare you with their bully tactics, but think with a clear head, then you've won. It will take time to get there. The mental and verbal abuse is weakening to the point you forget your own strength. But when you can slowly break out of the Kryptonite, you can begin again to find your strength and stay above the fray.

Not Responding is also a response.

- Huffpost.com

Zap Their Power

You can deflate the narcissist. Yes, you can. You may not feel empowered because the narcissist is a charming, expert, psychological abuser. They make you feel powerless, and when you show them your weakness, and then react to their insanity, they realize that their abuse of power is working.

Zapping their power is possible, but it may not happen quickly. The length of the relationship could determine how long it takes to heal your heart and soul. Chances are, you were the only one fighting to fix things: yourself, the relationship, them, and back to you again because they made you feel like everything wrong was your fault. Narcissists prey on people like us: the strong, the kind-hearted, the fixers, the level-headed, the confident and the most grounded. They are not those things, so they project everything they're not and everything they want to be on you. They work to break you down, so you feel like nothing and eventually completely numb. By the time it's all said and done, you don't know who you are anymore, what you're like, what you like; they've robbed you of you.

There is a way to de-power them, but it can only happen when you're stronger, and you've begun to heal. Before that, you may doubt yourself, and you will still try to please them. Once you've accepted that you've done all you can do, that they don't change and nothing you do can fix or change them, then you can begin to zap their power; if you still have to see and/or deal with them in some capacity.

Here's how it begins:

It will start with you realizing that they only want you if you can do something for them. When you stop giving in and realize that it's ok to say no or do what's best for you and not what's best for them, then the healing continues.

Their power is further zapped when you accept that their claims are yes, insane, and you're not the one that's crazy.

Furthermore, when you can stop caring about whether or not things are good between you two, when you care more about your feelings and not theirs, then you can see clearly. I'll warn you though, that is threatening to them, and they will make more outrageous claims about your "behavior." They will label you as erratic or say what you're doing is erratic. For example, my ex-husband happened to be driving behind me one evening after dropping off the children with him. When I didn't take the turn into my neighborhood as he expected I would, he freaked out. He called me immediately and said, "You didn't go home?" "Uh no," was my response, "How did you know that and why are you calling me asking me that?" He gave some lame excuse that he and my children happened to be driving by and they didn't see my car in the driveway. Uh, ok?!

The next day he emailed me asking if I was ok, that I had been acting strange lately, erratic in fact. I told him I'd never been better and yes, I was ok and that I didn't appreciate him tailing me. He then turned things around on me saying how crazy I was for saying and thinking that "a man with children in the car was tailing you."

They can't handle it when you care less about them and their feelings. They can't handle it when they're not your primary focus. When you have another love interest or the hint of one, they start to unravel because they've lost control of you and the relationship. Again, they begin to make outrageous claims and try to make you feel like it's you that's behaving badly.

Another clue that you're deflating them and zapping their power is when you just don't give a shit. You don't give a shit about what they do, what they say to you or about you or the bad things they tell your children about you.

You know you've healed completely when you can say to the narcissist, "Ok, you're right." Saying ok to EVERYTHING completely and eternally zaps their power. They want you to fight; they want you to react; they want you to yell and scream at them in the parking lot. Reacting solidifies their claims that you're the crazy one. Reacting gives them exactly what they want. Responding to their long empty emails with another long pointless email keeps the insanity going.

The best way to zap their power is just to agree. Say "Ok," even if it doesn't always fit. It totally confuses them and kills their next move and the next one after that.

They expect you to react because you're emotionally invested, but when you're healed, your emotions are no longer invested in them… your emotions are focused on you and your own personal peace. You begin to further protect yourself and learn how to better handle the abuser by blocking the abuse altogether.

Telling them "They're right" or not responding at all are other ways to shut them down. Most importantly, don't take it personally. In your heart, you know it's not you. If you haven't completely healed, believe me when I tell you, it's not you. Stay above the fray.

Let Them Be

The hardest part of leaving a narcissist is dealing with their emotional come-apart. Their temper tantrums are aimed at your heart and soul. You will want to fight back with equal emotion, words, physical blows, psychological weapons, etc. but you know that's what they want and you can't, so let them be.

The hardest part will be walking away when they say something insane, so let them be. Don't match them word for word, long email for long email, expletive for expletive. Loaded text for loaded text. Don't try to match them in any way whatsoever, let them be.

This will be excruciating to your core and soul, but it's better to let them be than to cause more drama and undue stress in your life.

They don't hear you. They don't see you. They don't care, so let them be. This is not easy for people like us. I've wanted so many times to kick him in the balls, punch his lights out, push him in front of a train (kidding, not kidding). I've wanted countless times to call him a "fucking idiot" to his face like, as he did me. It may feel better, and it will give you instant satisfaction but really, is it worth it?

Don't spend any of your neurons, organs, electrolytes, your precious thoughts, blood cells, chakras -whatever- on them. Don't give them any more of you. Let them be. Let them unravel on their own. You don't want to be anywhere near that because it doesn't suit you, who you are, and it certainly doesn't suit your image. Let them be, remember your ultimate goal is internal peace.

Turtles

My daughter and her friend dashed out the front door this morning yelling that they see a turtle in the road. Sure enough, there was a mid-sized turtle in the middle of our circle street. Their shouts startled him, and he did what turtles do, he recoiled. They begged me to let them "help him" across the road. We guessed he was trying to make his way back to the beautiful, majestic creek behind our circle of houses.

"I just feel like we should help him, Mommy." my daughter said.

I told my daughter and her friend to let him be and that he'll find his way. "Sometimes you just have to let nature be," I said. It was the natural thing to say, but the more I watched that turtle, the more I realized, the bigger epiphany of what was happening.

Many times in life, we try to force things or help things along when we just need to let them be. Nature is full of evolution, and it always finds its way eventually, if it's not interrupted by good intentioned humans. As a fixer, I've suffered from this all my life. I let things be after something has already been destroyed or ruined by my good intentions.

The girls followed my instruction to come back inside, but my middle son and I stood at the front glass door still staring at the turtle wondering what he would do. The turtle just sat there in the street. After a while, he poked his little head back out, but his legs were still tucked inside his shell. A car came around the circle, and we shouted to the driver, "Watch out for the turtle!" OMG! I wanted to cover my eyes, afraid the turtle would be smashed. The driver heard us… not really. He would've never heard us. He saw the turtle and avoided it.

I told my son, "We'll give the turtle 15 minutes. If he doesn't move, then we can go and help it." We walked away and continued our Saturday.

Five minutes later, we were back peering out the front door, delighted to see the turtle on the move!

"See, if you just leave him alone, he'll figure it out!" I said to my little middle one. "He's probably headed back to the creek." My son agreed and pointed out that the turtle's back was covered in caked mud. Yup, it sometimes takes turtles a long time to get where they're going, but they get there.

The turtle was energized with determination. You could tell by his speed. I thought I should snap a pic before he left our circle, which I did.

While this particular morning may have been just a compassionate turtle spotting to the children, it was a spotting of realization for me.

This is what I know for sure: We all are on a journey, some of us faster than others but each with will and determination. Big voices or unexpected surprises from behind sometimes halt us along the way and make us recoil until we get our footing again, but we continue when we're ready.

If we can figure out when to let others be and let nature evolve as its designed, then I think there is more peace in the world and definitely more harmony in our own souls. We can't force the actions of others. There is certainly a negative effect of our good intentions. Evolving daily is about knowing when to walk away and let the turtle be. With a change in perspective on the lesson, it applies to our overall life, or situations we need to keep our distance from. Sometimes the turtle is that dream we want to help and hurry up. Once it's in the street, sometimes you need to let it go at its own pace.

Will it Ever Stop?

I don't have an answer to that question. I have no idea, and I often wondered if it ever will just stop. I don't know. I expect it won't because I've finally stepped outside of the situation, and I've created strict boundaries. I'm sticking to them, which is increasing his level of anger, but I don't give a damn! I've been more forcefully resistant to the narcissism and mental abuse. I've been clear about what I won't do, and I've plainly communicated that to him; and he doesn't like it one bit. I can write that with a smile on my face. There was a time my face would be crinkled and frowned from just thinking about it, but now, now I can write about this with a little smirk because I'm mentally healthier.

Dealing and living with him seemed easier under his thumb as long as I drowned in his existence. As long as I didn't put up a fuss, things were ok. As long as I went along with and just kept my mouth shut, and agreed with his false sense of reality, and believed his lies about me, then things were ok. But I couldn't keep my mouth shut anymore! I'd had enough!

I don't think it will ever stop, because they don't see the necessity of what's best for the children and they're inadequate co-parents. Their only mission during the divorce and the aftermath, during the marriage, during the relationship, is to punish you for what they think you've done to them. Everything is a volley even if, in your head and mind, you're not fighting or competing with them in any way. What angers them is that you begin to care less about pleasing them, less about what they want, and less about giving them attention. They can't handle that, so they try to stay relevant; they try to stay present in your world… not for the children's sake, but for their own sake. They have to matter, and they have to have some sense of control. They need your undivided attention on all things "them," but they are unwilling to give to you what they demand of you. They are unwilling to give you attention; they are unwilling to help you; they are unwilling to do something meaningful for you or the children if they don't see or believe there's a benefit in it for them.

My children and I moved out of state, back to Austin, Texas, during our separation. I thought I was far enough away from the abuse. Even though there was distance, the visits, the plans, the arrangements, everything was full of DRAMA! I remember the first visit, he and I were cordial enough that I suggested he stay with us in our apartment so the children could spend more time with him and he could save money. As soon as the children went to bed, he tried to pick a fight about something from the past. I was strong enough that I told him there was no fighting in our house and I had moved away from that. I kicked him out. He had to hail a cab, find a hotel, the whole nine yards at 11 o'clock at night. I didn't care. That was the beginning of my creating boundaries, but I eventually moved back to Alabama. That experiment is covered in another upcoming book.

Even though he was miles away, he still would do everything he could to rupture me again and again. I tried to Ebay sell some furniture pieces we agreed to sell. The baby crib sold, but he refused to dismantle and ship it. He eventually took it apart but he hid it so no one could find it. I had no money, zero dollars in my bank account, no job, and was trying to raise and feed three children. He didn't care about the children, obviously. He only cared about punishing me because I had done something without his *permission*.

He keeps coming, and he keeps coming with some kind of bullshit. He doesn't stop. It's always something, and it's always something that I've done wrong. Whether it's my parenting, packing the children's bags, why I've said no to something, ugh!! It goes on and on. There's no point in trying to have a meaningful conversation, and there's no point in even having the conversation anymore. We can't. We can't even converse face to face. That was a tough reality for me to accept. I'm a communicator. I believe I'm a fairly reasonable person and an open-minded thinker. I like talking it out, and I like working through something towards a positive resolution. But narcissists are not reasonable, and it is impossible for them to see that they may be wrong about something.

Several of my friends are in and out of court, years after their divorce, because their narcissistic ex is dragging them back in front of a judge for something bogus. My ex is also suing me right now. If they believe that something is your fault, and in their mind, it's always your fault, then no, it probably won't stop. If you have children together, it's worse.

If you don't have children together, count your blessings and severe any ties you still have. Get rid of anything, any artifact, anything that reminds you of the person. Chances are they'll want it back anyway. Don't expect to get any of your things back either. My ex still has my bridal portrait that he didn't pay for and had nothing to do with, but refuses to return. I let it go five years ago. I believe that's his way of trying to hold on to yet another piece of me.

They can't let go. So, will it ever stop? Probably not, but what will stop over time is your care and concern about it and your ability to **create, maintain, and remain steadfast in your boundaries.**

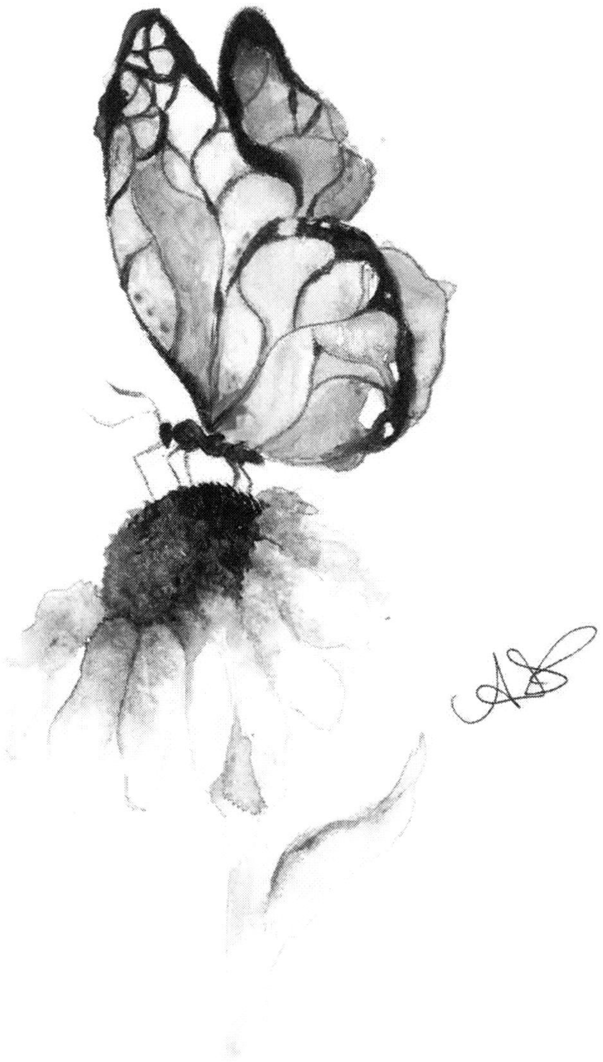

There's no passion to be found playing small in settling for a life that is less than the one you are capable of living

- Nelson Mandela

Hope and Healing

There's no timeframe for healing your heart and soul. It just takes time. I don't know that it has a lot to do with the amount of time you endured the abuse, but I do know that it takes patience, forgiving yourself and self-care. I was married almost ten years, divorced for seven, and I still find myself crying occasionally when I read what I experienced. My tears are different than before though. They aren't sad tears. The tears now are in disbelief of what I endured and actually survived.

Speaking out will make a huge difference and aid in healing. I might have healed sooner if I wasn't silent for as long as I was. Speaking out was relief and encouraging. Speaking out aligned me with a community of other abused survivors who had stories just as important, and even more severe than my own. The results of speaking out have been shocking and enlightening at the same time.

I recently posted on Facebook that my ex called me a "fucking idiot" to my face. I'm mostly private and don't use social media to express personal issues, but this time, I had to tell someone. I remembered my bravery and I was drained from being silent. I'm joyfully relieved God prompted me to post. The response and outpouring of love and encouragement from my Facebook community was absolutely humbling! I learned that many others out there are enduring and have endured narcissistic abuse. Some sent me private messages, telling me their own stories of verbal and psychological abuse, and it is unbelievable. It made me realize how important it is to speak out.

Healing may spark a myriad of emotions, and you may jump from joy to anger in an instant as you're working to clear your head and heart, but you will find hope again. You will continue to sort through it by distancing yourself, creating boundaries, and holding steadfast to them.

You may be upset with yourself for seeming weak or out of control of your emotions. You may doubt yourself, your self-worth, your ability to be a dynamic person, and your inner strength may be damaged, but know that this has nothing to do with your core and the person who you really are.

You are a child of God. You are strong. You are beautiful. You are light. You are love. You are full of life and have so much of it still to live. When you begin to doubt, just read this chapter over and over and pray.

Praying and being in sync with your spiritual life will also help you heal. God gives you strength and exactly what you need for the days and moments when you can't stand on your own. That gift may translate into a quick text or phone call from a friend. God's gift of strength could be a friend's vulnerability by opening their heart to you to share their story. Sometimes, just being able to converse and vent validates your perspective, giving you calm until you regain focus.

There is hope and sun outside the cloud of the distress of a narcissist relationship. There is clarity of heart, soul, and mind, and there is peace. I'm living proof. You will be able to deal with the narcissist on a different level than before because your internal mental power will be re-energized and strengthened. You will be able to walk away when they're verbally attacking you and, at some point, you'll be able to laugh at how insane their behavior has become. Remember, their motivation comes from your reaction and you physically and/or verbally reacting to their lashings. If you don't react, you've deflated them. Rather than give them your energy, save it for your children and yourself. Invest that same energy in healing your being. You've been through a lot, and you are not alone.

Resources

FindingYouAgain.org

For the Love of Eryk: Surviving Divorce, Parental Alienation and Life After, Rod McCall

Will I Ever Be Free of You? How to Navigate a High Conflict Divorce from a Narcissist and Heal Your Family, Dr. Karyl McBride.

The Challenge of Co- Parenting with a Narcissist, Alex Myles, Elephant Journal

Don't Sweat the Small Stuff and It's All Small Stuff, Richard Carlson

You're Not Going Crazy. 15 Signs You're a Victim of Gaslighting, Alethia Luna, Lone Wolf

11 Signs of Gaslighting in a Relationship, Stephanie Sarkis, Ph.D., Psychology Today

Option B: Facing Adversity, Building Resilience and Finding Joy, Sheryl Sandberg and Adam Grant

About the Author
Catenya McHenry

Catenya McHenry is an every-day woman: a single mom of three just trying to get out the door on time! In her professional life, she's an entrepreneur and sought-after TV host, writer, producer, and wardrobe ReStylist, making regular television appearances as a guest on dozens of top-rated shows.

She's also the inventor of the patent-pending SoleMate Sox magnetic socks, staying paired on laundry day, eliminating lost socks.

Born and raised in Los Angeles, California, the hub of film and fashion, Catenya was destined to be in the mix. Her dad owned a video production company and from there, her love of stories and storytelling ignited. Catenya began her journey as a TV news reporter in Lafayette, Louisiana. Within eight months, she was advancing to an education reporter position in Austin, Texas and later became their morning show anchor. As a news broadcaster, Catenya has logged thousands of stories and TV appearances for all the major networks, including NBC, CNN, ABC, CBS, FOX and the CW.

Catenya's constant curiosity and insatiable desire for the next challenge gave her the bravery to flip her skills and quickly ascend to corporate executive level, becoming a PR executive, communications and crisis-communications expert, media trainer as well as a marketing expert. Catenya later used that experience to launch two PR firms and a video production company.

Never satisfied with just one thing at a time, Catenya's love of film and the creative process prompted her to dabble in the industry. She is SAG credited for her principal roles in two films, *Miss Congeniality* and *The Life of David Gale*. She's also appeared in dozens of industrial commercials for TV, corporate, and print campaigns and is the voice-over talent in a host of radio commercials.

Although Catenya has been blessed with wonderful opportunities in her life, she's now intently focused on a more authentic life that exudes her passions. She recently rededicated her professional life to taking on projects with purpose, truth, and deeper meaning.

Real stories, real people, and *Married to a Narcissist* evolved from that rededication. During her metamorphosis, Catenya realized she had a catalog of writings and a story to tell. Exhausted from being silent about the continual abuse, she courageously penned her book. "I learned to be silent and cry on the inside. My heart cried. My nerves cried. My blood cried," she writes. "My soul became mute because the narcissism was deafening. The only thing listening was my journal, as recorded in *Journaling the Journey*," Part One of her book. "Writing it was not hard because it was my reality."

Married to A Narcissist is for those who have no one to tell. Catenya writes, "This is for those who cry inwardly. This is for those who, like me, don't know that it is okay to leave. This is for those who believe "till death do us part" means physical death. 'Death do us part' could also mean death of your soul."

Catenya can now add Author to her professional credentials. She has already begun writing her second book.

Aknowledgements

This book took on life and essentially wrote itself. It's been a 17-year process of dealing with abuse by an extreme narcissist. Along the way, God gave me divine angels who helped me heal a little at time. I'd like to pour out my heart of gratitude to them.

If you know me, you are aware that accepting help is extremely difficult for me. Most often, I try to do things myself and then call in the cavalry only when it's too late or close to it. I also don't like attention, even though I love being in front of the camera. My anxiety about asking for help makes me feel like I'm bothering people or imposing. So, when I express that I'm so grateful for everything and all the ways that I've been blessed, the gratitude comes from the deepest part of me.

When I left Alabama during our separation and moved back to Austin, Texas, I vehemently vowed to never return to Alabama- what I called *"the god-forsaken place where everything fell apart."* But in time, I reluctantly returned. I believe God only needed me to exercise my faith. He took care of the rest. Within two weeks of relocating, I met Chris. Sent from heaven, she became someone my soul connected with.

Thank you, Chris, for being the love, light, and support I needed as a single Mom, as a woman, and as a person who was struggling on the inside but still trying to hold it together. Thank you for understanding, seeing my hurt, and knowing the right thing to say and/or do at any given moment. Thank you for always being available to step in when I had those, *"oh god, you won't believe what he did now"* or *"what am I going to do, he didn't show up"* moments. Thank you for making it so easy to call you. Thank you for letting me just talk, and thank you most of all for intently listening. Thank you for caring for my children the same way I do and thank you for passing along the words God gave you. They are still with me. You didn't know you were helping me write this book, but you did. I love you!

Thank you to my network of sisterhood, Sheila, Connie, Suzie, and Christina, for being beautiful strength and empowerment! Thank you for supporting me and just being who you are, for you have helped me heal.

To my beautiful cousin Mai, thank you, for reminding me of my own strength and encouraging me to keep going to see this book through. Thank you for your ideas and vision, and most of all, your ability to help me see past what's right in front. Thank you for speaking out loud the important lesson of being 'patient with the process.'

To my cousin, Aja, this project would not make sense without your visionary and artistic intelligence! Your artwork gives this book cohesion, telling a compelling story that I know women and men will connect with. Your beautiful talent is undeniably special. Thank you so much for listening, for paying attention to the pain, and translating it into images that will move audiences worldwide. Thank you for unequivocally being willing to share your talents with me and thank you for being willing to freely give of yourself. You have captured the raw truth and the emotional essence of what so many have endured. I love you dearly and love that we are family!

Thank you, Jim, for calling me nearly every day throughout some of the toughest bouts of this. Thank you for being excited when good things happened and thank you for making me laugh when I needed to de-stress. I love you!

Thank you to my sister, Marika, for reminding me that I'm not crazy and for reassuring me that what I was experiencing was not right. Thank you for standing by my side and thank you for the regular bitch sessions. They help us both stay sane. I love you so much!

Thank you to my brothers for helping me where you could and doing the best that you could to help me and the children during some of our weakest moments.

Thank you, Dad, for standing up and fighting for me! Thank you for being patient when I didn't want you to say anything to my ex, fearing his backlash. Thank you for holding your words for my sake- until you couldn't anymore. Thank you for listening anytime I need to talk and thank you for your Godly wisdom and sound advice. There have been many days when I could not find my footing in my faith and I struggled to understand why I was being tried and tested in the way that I was. You have continued to help me see beyond the engulfing turmoil and you lift me when I run out of strength to see beyond my tears.

In good times and in bad, your solution is to talk to God about it. Thank you for praying whenever things are troublesome. Your extraordinary example is a testament to the incredible man you are and I'm overjoyed, overwhelmed, and richly blessed that you are my Dad my children's grandfather. Together, you and Mom were incredible parents. I know Mom is smiling from heaven.

To Melanie, my amazing editor and publisher, thank you for making this goal attainable. I had no idea what I was doing or how to make this collection of writings an actual book. Thank you for giving me confidence to become an author! From our first conversation, I felt like I'd known you for much longer than just the first five minutes of our phone call. Thank you for being warm, engaging and interested in my story. Thank you for being honest about the direction and thank you for being patient and when I challenged various aspects of this project. You truly have a gift and a love for people. It shows in every communication, and we had A LOT, and it shows in the way you handle the most treacherous pieces of what you do. Thank you for sharing your talent, expertise and most of all your heart. Although this is your job, I believe you've gone beyond the profession and inserted your passion.

To anyone else that I've not mentioned by name, you know my heart. Know that I love you!

Printed in Great Britain
by Amazon